THE
BEST
AMERICAN
POETRY
2007

◇　◇　◇

Heather McHugh, Editor

David Lehman, Series Editor

SCRIBNER POETRY

NEW YORK   LONDON   TORONTO   SYDNEY

SCRIBNER POETRY
A Division of Simon & Schuster, Inc.
1230 Avenue of the Americas
New York, NY 10020

First Scribner edition September 2007

Manufactured in the United States of America

1   3   5   7   9   10   8   6   4   2

Library of Congress Control Number: 2005049982

ISBN-13: 978-0-7432-9972-5
ISBN-10: 0-7432-9972-8
ISBN-13: 978-0-7432-9973-2 (Pbk)
ISBN-10: 0-7432-9973-6 (Pbk)

CONTENTS

David Lehman was born in New York City in 1948. He is the author of seven books of poems, most recently *When a Woman Loves a Man* (Scribner, 2005). Among his nonfiction books are *The Last Avant-Garde: The Making of the New York School of Poets* (Anchor, 1999) and *The Perfect Murder* (Michigan, 2000). He edited *Great American Prose Poems: From Poe to the Present,* which appeared from Scribner in 2003. He teaches writing and literature in the graduate writing program of the New School in New York City and offers an undergraduate course each fall on "Great Poems" at NYU. He edited the new edition of *The Oxford Book of American Poetry,* a one-volume comprehensive anthology of poems from Anne Bradstreet to the present. Lehman has collaborated with James Cummins on a book of sestinas, *Jim and Dave Defeat the Masked Man* (Soft Skull), and with Judith Hall on a "p'lem," or "play poem," combining words and images, *Poetry Forum* (Bayeux Arts). He initiated the *Best American Poetry* series in 1988 and received a Guggenheim Fellowship a year later. He lives in New York City and in Ithaca, New York.

FOREWORD

by David Lehman

◇ ◇ ◇

A parody, even a merciless one, is not necessarily an act of disrespect. Far from it. Poets parody other poets for the same reason they write poems in imitation (or opposition): as a way of engaging with a distinctive manner or voice. A really worthy parody is implicitly an act of homage.

Some great poets invite parody. Wordsworth's "Resolution and Independence" prompted Lewis Carroll to pen "The White Knight's Song" in *Through the Looking Glass*. In a wonderful poem, J. K. Stephen alludes to the sestet of a famous Wordsworth sonnet ("The world is too much with us") to dramatize the wide discrepancy between Wordsworth at his best and worst. "At certain times / Forth from the heart of thy melodious rhymes, / The form and pressure of high thoughts will burst," Stephen writes. "At other times—good Lord! I'd rather be / Quite unacquainted with the ABC / Than write such hopeless rubbish as thy worst."

Among the moderns, T. S. Eliot reliably triggers off the parodist. Wendy Cope brilliantly reduced *The Waste Land* to five limericks ("The Thames runs, bones rattle, rats creep; / Tiresias fancies a peep— / A typist is laid, / A record is played— / Wei la la. After this it gets deep") while Eliot's late sententious manner stands behind Henry Reed's "Chard Whitlow" with its throat-clearing assertions ("As we get older we do not get any younger"). In a recent (2006) episode of *The Simpsons* on television, Lisa Simpson assembles a poem out of torn-up fragments, and attributes it to Moe the bartender. The title: "Howling at a Concrete Moon." The inspiration: *The Waste Land*. The cigar-chewing editor of *American Poetry Perspectives* barks into the phone, "Genius. Pay him nothing and put him on the cover."

Undoubtedly the most parodied of all poems is Matthew Arnold's "Dover Beach," which has long served graduation speakers and Polonius-wannabes as a touchstone. Arnold turned forty-five in 1867, the year the poem first appeared in print. Here it is:

Dover Beach

The sea is calm to-night.
The tide is full, the moon lies fair
Upon the straits; — on the French coast the light
Gleams and is gone; the cliffs of England stand,
Glimmering and vast, out in the tranquil bay.
Come to the window, sweet is the night-air!

Only, from the long line of spray
Where the sea meets the moon-blanch'd land,
Listen! you hear the grating roar
Of pebbles which the waves draw back, and fling,
At their return, up the high strand,
Begin, and cease, and then again begin,
With tremulous cadence slow, and bring
The eternal note of sadness in.

Sophocles long ago
Heard it on the Aegean, and it brought
Into his mind the turbid ebb and flow
Of human misery; we
Find also in the sound a thought,
Hearing it by this distant northern sea.

The Sea of Faith
Was once, too, at the full, and round earth's shore
Lay like the folds of a bright girdle furl'd.
But now I only hear
Its melancholy, long, withdrawing roar,
Retreating, to the breath
Of the night-wind, down the vast edges drear
And naked shingles of the world.

Ah, love, let us be true
To one another! for the world, which seems
To lie before us like a land of dreams,
So various, so beautiful, so new,
Hath really neither joy, nor love, nor light,
Nor certitude, nor peace, nor help for pain;

And we are here as on a darkling plain
Swept with confused alarms of struggle and flight,
Where ignorant armies clash by night.

The greatness of this poem lies in the way it transforms the painting of a scene into a vision of "eternal sadness" and imminent danger. Moonlight and the English Channel contemplated from atop the white cliffs of Dover by a man and woman in love would seem a moment for high romance, and a reaffirmation of vows as a prelude to sensual pleasure. But "Dover Beach," while remaining a love poem, is not about the couple so much as it is about a crisis in faith and a foreboding of dreadful things to come. It communicates the anxiety of an age in which scientific hypotheses, such as Darwin's theory of evolution, combined with philosophical skepticism to throw into doubt the comforting belief in an all-knowing and presumably benevolent deity. The magnificent closing peroration, as spoken by the poet to his beloved, has the quality of a prophecy darkly fulfilled. Genocidal violence, perpetrated by "ignorant armies," marked the last century, and it is undeniable that we today face a continuing crisis in faith and confidence. Seldom have our chief institutions of church and state seemed as vulnerable as they do today with, on the one side, a citizenry that seems alienated to the extent that it is educated, and on the other side, enemies as implacable and intolerant as they are medieval and reactionary.

Though traditional in its means, "Dover Beach" is, in its spirit and its burden of sense, a brutally modern poem, and among the first to be thus designated. "Arnold showed an awareness of the emotional conditions of modern life which far exceeds that of any other poet of his time," Lionel Trilling observed. "He spoke with great explicitness and directness of the alienation, isolation, and excess of consciousness leading to doubt which are, as so much of later literature testifies, the lot of modern man." And Trilling goes on to note that in "Dover Beach" in particular the diction is perfect and the verse moves "in a delicate crescendo of lyricism" to the "great grim simile" that lends the poem's conclusion its desperation and its pathos.

While perfect for the right occasion, a recitation of the poem is, because of its solemnity, absurd in most circumstances, as when, in the 2001 movie *The Anniversary Party,* the Kevin Kline character recites the closing lines from memory in lieu of an expected lighthearted toast, and the faces of the other characters change from pleasure to confusion and alarm. Inspired responses to "Dover Beach" spring to mind. In "The

Dover Bitch," Anthony Hecht presents the situation of Arnold's poem from the woman's point of view. She rather resents being treated "as a sort of mournful cosmic last resort," brought all the way from London for a honeymoon and receiving a sermon instead of an embrace. Tom Clark lampoons "Dover Beach" more farcically. His poem begins as Arnold's does, but where in the third line of the original "the French coast" gleams in the distance, in Clark's poem light syrup drips on "the French toast," and the poem continues in the spirit of "crashing ignorance." A third example is John Brehm's "Sea of Faith," which Robert Bly selected for the 1999 edition of *The Best American Poetry*. Here a college student wonders whether the body of water named in the poem's title exists in geographical fact. The student's ignorance seems to confirm Arnold's gloomy vision, but it also spurs the instructor to a more generous response. After all, who has not felt the unspoken wish for an allegorical sea in which one can swim and reemerge "able to believe in everything, faithful / and unafraid to ask even the simplest of questions, / happy to have them simply answered"?

Poets like to parody "Dover Beach" because the poem takes itself so very seriously and because Arnold's wording sticks in the mind. But not everyone agrees on what lesson we should draw from this case. The poet Edward Dorn, author of *Gunslinger* and other estimable works, called "Dover Beach" the "greatest single poem ever written in the English language." What amazed Dorn was that it should be Arnold who wrote it. According to Dorn, Arnold "wrote volume after volume of lousy, awful poetry." The anomaly "proves that you should never give up," Dorn added. If Arnold with his "pedestrian mind" could write "Dover Beach," then "anybody could do it."

I have dwelled on "Dover Beach" as an object of irreverence not only because the parodic impulse, which informs so many contemporary poems (including some in this volume), is misunderstood and sometimes unfairly derogated, but also because of a superb counterexample that came to my attention this year. In his novel *Saturday* (2005), Ian McEwan makes earnest use of "Dover Beach" as a rich, unironic emblem of the values of Western Civilization. It is not the only such emblem in the book. There are Bach's *Goldberg Variations* and Samuel Barber's *Adagio for Strings,* to which the book's neurosurgeon hero listens when operating, and there is the surgeon's knife, the antithesis of the thug's switchblade. But a reading aloud of "Dover Beach" in the most extreme of circumstances marks the turning point in the plot of this novel whose subject is terror and terrorism.

Set in London on a day of massive antiwar demonstrations, *Saturday* centers on a car accident that pits Henry, the surgeon, against Baxter, a local crime boss. Henry gets the better of Baxter in the confrontation, and in retaliation the gangster and a henchman mount an assault on the surgeon and his family in their posh London home. Baxter systematically humiliates Henry's grown daughter, an aspiring poet, forcing her to strip off all her clothing in front of her horrified parents, brother, and grandfather. But the young woman's just-published first book of poems, lying on the coffee table, catches Baxter's eye, and he commands her to read from it. She opens the book but recites "Dover Beach" from memory instead—with startling consequences. The transformation of the gangster is abrupt and total. In a flash he goes "from lord of terror to amazed admirer," a state in which it becomes possible for the family to overpower him. Thus does poetry, in effect, disarm the brute and lead to the family's salvation.

With the restoration of safety and order, McEwan allows himself a little joke at the expense of both Matthew Arnold and his own protagonist. The surgeon tells his daughter of her choice of poem, "I didn't think it was one of your best." The joke, a good one, reminds us of the poem's complicated cultural status: revered, iconic, but also mildly desecrated, like a public statue exposed to pigeons and graffiti artists. But McEwan has already made his more significant point. Just as the instructor in John Brehm's poem can find himself yearning for an escape to an allegorical Sea of Faith, so I believe we all secretly think of poetry, this art that we love unreasonably, as somehow antidotal to malice and vice, cruelty and wrath. We know it isn't so, and yet we persist in writing poems that shoulder the burden of conscience. In *The Best American Poetry 2007* you will find poems in a variety of tonal registers—by such poets as Denise Duhamel, Robert Hass, Frederick Seidel, Brian Turner, and Joe Wenderoth—that address subjects ranging from "Bush's War" to the "language police," from the decapitation of an American citizen in Iraq to the overthrow of the shah of Iran.

For such a poem to gain entry into this volume, it had to meet exceptionally high criteria. Heather McHugh, the editor of *The Best American Poetry 2007,* sets store, she told an interviewer, by wordplay, puns, rhymes, the hidden life of words, "the *is* in the wish, the *or* in the word. No word-fun should be left undone." McHugh has spoken with cutting eloquence against glib and simplistic poems by well-meaning citizens: "So much contemporary American poetry is deadly serious, reeking of the NPR virtues: back-to-the-earth soup eaten fresh from the woodstove, all its spices listed, then some admirable thoughts to put to paper when we get home. Hey, Romanticism isn't dead—it's simply being turned to public pap. Against that tedium, a little unholiness comes as a big relief—the skeptic skeleton, the romping rump." But it should also be noted that McHugh herself, for all the wit and wordplay in her poems, has written a poem that I would not hesitate to characterize as powerful, earnest, and political: "What He Said" (1994), which culminates in a definition of poetry as what the heretical philosopher Giordano Bruno, when burned at the stake, "thought, but did not say," with an iron mask placed on his face, as the flames consumed him.

In his poem "My Heart," Frank O'Hara wrote, "I'm not going to cry all the time / nor shall I laugh all the time, / I don't prefer one 'strain' to another." By temperament and inclination I favor both kinds of poems—the kind that celebrates and the kind that criticizes; the kind that affirms a vow and the kind that makes merry; the poem of high seriousness that would save the world and the poem of high hilarity that would mock the pretensions of saviors. I believe, with Wordsworth, that the poet's first obligation is always to give pleasure, and I would argue, too, that a poem exhibiting the comic spirit can be every bit as serious as a poem devoid of laughter. The poems McHugh gathers in this volume are unafraid to confront the world in its contradictory guises and moods. The unlikely cast of characters includes authentic geniuses from far-flung places: Catullus, Leonardo, Voltaire, Kant, the lyricist Lorenz Hart. There are sonnets and prose poems, a set of haiku and a country-western song, a double abecedarian and a lover's quarrel with a famous Frost poem. And there are poems that take a mischievous delight in the English language as an organic thing, a living system, full of puns that reveal truths just as jokes and errors served Freud: as ways the mind inadvertently discloses itself. Some of these poems are very funny, and need no further justification. "The human race has one really effective weapon, and that is laughter," Mark Twain remarked.

There is a dangerous if common misconception that a political poem, or *any* poem that aspires to move the hearts and minds of men and women, must be reducible to a paraphrase the length of a slogan, be it that "war is hell" or that "hypocrisy is rampant" or that "it is folly to launch a major invasion without a postwar strategy in place." For such sentiments, an editorial or a letter to the editor would serve as the proper vehicle. We want something more complicated and more lasting from poetry. An anecdote from the biography of Oscar Hammerstein II, who succeeded Lorenz Hart as Richard Rodgers's lyricist, may help here. When Stephen

Sondheim, then in high school, appealed for advice to Hammerstein, his mentor, the latter criticized a song the young man had written: "This doesn't say anything." Sondheim recalls answering defensively, "What does 'Oh, What a Beautiful Mornin' ' say?" With a firmness Sondheim would not forget, Hammerstein responded, "Oh, it says a lot."

The parodist in each of us will continue to enjoy a secret laugh at "Dover Beach." But we also know that people who live in newspapers die for want of what there is in Arnold's poem and in great poetry in general. Real poetry sustains us. György Faludy, the Hungarian poet and Resistance hero, died on September 1, 2006, sixty-seven years to the day after the Nazis invaded Poland. Faludy attacked Hitler in a poem but managed to escape to the United States and served in the American army during World War II. He wasn't nearly so fortunate when he returned to Hungary following the war. For three years, from 1950 to 1953, the Soviets imprisoned Faludy in Recsk, Hungary's Stalinist concentration camp. He endured terrible hardships, but even without a pen he wrote, using the bristle of a broom to inscribe his verses in blood on toilet paper. He had to write. Poetry was keeping him alive. He recited his poems and made fellow prisoners memorize them. The imagination created hope, and the heart committed its lines to memory. When Faludy called his prose book about the years in the camp "My Happy Days in Hell," it was with obvious irony, but it also hinted at his faith. He had listened to the melancholy, long withdrawing roar of the sea, survived the shock, and outlived the Soviet occupation just as his beloved Danube River had done.

Heather McHugh was born in San Diego, California, in 1948. She was raised in Virginia and educated at Harvard University. She is the Milliman Distinguished Writer-in-Residence at the University of Washington in Seattle and has held visiting appointments at the University of California at Berkeley and at the Writers' Workshop at the University of Iowa. She regularly visits the low-residency creative writing program at Warren Wilson College near Asheville, North Carolina. Her books of poetry include *Eyeshot* (Wesleyan University Press, 2003), *The Father of the Predicaments* (Wesleyan, 1999), *Hinge & Sign: Poems 1968–1993* (Wesleyan, 1994), and *Dangers* (Houghton Mifflin, 1977). Her collection of literary essays is entitled *Broken English: Poetry and Partiality* (1993). *Glottal Stop: 101 Poems by Paul Celan,* which she translated in collaboration with her husband, Nikolai Popov, was published in the fall of 2000. Her translation of the poems of Jean Follain was published by Princeton in 1981, and her version of Euripides' *Cyclops* by Oxford University Press in 2003. She has received fellowships and grants from the Lila Wallace Foundation, United States Artists, the National Endowment for the Arts, and the Guggenheim Foundation, and in 1999 was named a chancellor of the Academy of American Poets. She was elected a member of the American Academy of Arts and Sciences in 2000.

INTRODUCTION

by Heather McHugh

◇   ◇   ◇

Poetry attracted me in the first place, fifty years ago, because (half gasp half gape) it seemed constitutively thunderstruck, wonderstruck. The oddity and opportunity of verbal life seemed not just a poem's object but its fundamental subject: In a poem, theme and instrument could not be told apart. Except insofar as verve or the vernacular refresh it, daily life wants language chiefly for a tool of will, to note the sorely needed or the merely known. But as soon as systems of words are wielded by intentions only, predictable and paraphrasable, they begin to bore me. A logophiliacal hunger craves amazement. And words can blaze!—most brightly where (like fires) their logs are interlaid with airs. They can flow—or flock—or fluster! From their arrangement in measures, uncontainability pours forth. . . . (And so it is with us: We can't contain ourselves.)

My lifelong romance with literary objects began not with the wish to say some*thing,* but with the hope to say some*how.* Maugham cited his stammer as his major influence: Had he never stammered, he tells us, he might (like his brothers) have gone to Cambridge, become a professor, and now and then published "a dreary book on French literature." For my part, I began to read and write poems because in company I constantly misspoke. (Better to scratch than to spit.)

Fond of the textures of a text, the matter of a letter, I've always gravitated toward ideograms, letterforms, literary graphics, and kinetics, the white space composing the poetic frame. I'm a logic-and-structure addict but I'm also swayable by a passage's sonic architectonics. I hope my heart is smart; my brain knows braille. I bring six senses to the enterprise, or seven: because poetry is (as Poe said) "not a purpose, but a passion."

In my own lifetime of reading (the pre-postmodern and beyond), the aphorism "Well-spoken is half-sung" has routinely been treated as if it were reversible: as if "well-sung is half-spoken" might equally be plausible. It isn't. Half-spoken's a broken wheel. The muse rides home on music. Poetry cares for the *means* of the meaning business.

I had hoped with this anthology to include examples from the provocative fields of Web life today—various sonic and kinetic and electronic poetries. I wanted, that is, to add a CD; alas, it was not permitted. So I make do with mere mention of estimable energy sources in other media—online magazines like *Poems that Go* and the legendary Electronic Poetry Center at the University of Buffalo (hats off to Loss Pequeño Glazier). There's lively invention going on in digital poetry, visual poetry, algorithmic poetry, interactive works, the treatment and edition of raw material from text generators, and more. These irrepressible media have logophiliacal premises too, and as great talents rise among the experimenters, you'll find them represented at such sites.

By contrast, poems in this present volume originated in relatively conventional print and online journals. They have in common their having moved me, one way or another—first individually and then, as the year proceeded, in sequences (for they were assembled under terms of time and auspices of alphabet). Convincing curves and conversations emerged, and some of the poems I had originally chosen turned out not to have a place in the upcropping force fields. Uncanny links became apparent— one poem speaks of unfacings, the next of beheadings. "I re-ink" near the end of one poem leads to "I typed" at the outset of the next; "Gods again, or coming" comes just before "Comma of God." The sequences began to have their way with me, and I let them. "A flaming prick" precedes a "valentine." So be it. As in life.

Incidents may be accidents—the way things fall, the case of all that is, with its roots in the Latin *cadere*. But sequences grow consequential. The year unfolded, and refashioned what I found compelling. (It seems no accident to me now that "The Art of Breathing" should appear at the beginning: I'm told that the Haida use the same verb to mean both breathing and the making of poetry.) Near the end of the anthology, you'll find in one poem the perilune of a pupil and, in the next, a tally of the eye blinks of a beheadee. The collection closes (by grace of Zinnes and the letter *Z*) with "let it be / and behind it all / you will see / the globe . . . / undreamed of but beheld." In the blink of an eye, at every turn, I was beholden.

The most powerful poems (leaping from word to word, from line to line) will also leap from writer to reader, singer to swayer, life to life. They may not shout out loud or spend a million on a twenty-second spot. They may not craze a crowd on *Letterman*—yet the quietest can shine, the smallest tap into an uncontainability . . . that's why we go to them. Like other sorts of matter, they contain unfathomable space. Even in a year in which I overdosed on poetry, I now and then could still be zapped by somebody's design, zinged by somebody's instrument, zithered by somebody's wit. This collection suggests (as does the sequence of such collections) how variously glittering are American journals today. Of course a *jour*, or a year (a poem itself!), is like Lichtenberg's mirror: If an ass looks into it, you can't expect an apostle to look out. And bestov, schmestov—(let your work be kept to yourself nine years, says Horace!)—this is only a glimpse; the present is lost on us. Through everything let's keep one eye on Dickinson, for sheer perspective:

> Fame is the one that does not stay—
> Its occupant must die
> Or out of sight of Estimate
> Ascend incessantly—
> Or be that most insolvent thing
> A Lightning in the Germ—
> Electrical the embryo—
> But we demand the Flame. (#1475)

THE
BEST
AMERICAN
POETRY
2007

◇   ◇   ◇

KAZIM ALI

The Art of Breathing

◊　◊　◊

Do you lose yourself
in the cave of endless breath,

the moment you don't want to know yourself,
soaring or frightened—

Says Arjuna on the battlefield, throwing down his bow,
"I refuse to fight my cousins and kin."

Says dark-blue Krishna, "These are only tricks and metaphor,
selfishness and separation, your cheapness and rage."

So when Karna's chariot wheel breaks,
and he stumbles down to fix it,

Krishna whips the horses faster toward them. "Shoot!" he yells
to Arjuna, "You can destroy your own alienation if you do it!"

Arjuna pulls his arrow back and looks long through the sight
at his secret brother, the broken wheel—

from *Barrow Street*

JEANNETTE ALLÉE

Crimble of Staines

◊　◊　◊

You're back in motherbickered
England dumb with brick
& viper typists.
Such organized fear: rigidity as fetish
Sphincter sphunct filthiness in wainscoted ways.

Jolly ol' brims with againstness
"Anti-clockwise"—"ante-natal" if you will—
The "crumbling masonry" of
Your "anti-relationship structure" you once called it before
You went away. Such negativity in names:
Wormwood Scrubs as prison, animal park Whipsnade
The motorshop Crimble of Staines
Kidney pie tastes like potty
Cheat never equals cheated upon.

After you left me, I brought a barrister
Besotted—blotto—up to my rooms
Is this how they do it I kept wondering,
Dull as cotton batting, without love?
In his garden variety serpentry he left
On our bodgy bed—a wrunkled skin—still crawling, crawling.

from *FIELD*

Scumble

◇ ◇ ◇

What if I were turned on by seemingly innocent words such as "scumble," "pinky," or "extrapolate?"

What if I maneuvered conversation in the hope that others would pronounce these words?

Perhaps the excitement would come from the way the other person touched them lightly and carelessly with his tongue.

What if "of" were such a hot button?

"Scumble of bushes."

What if there were a hidden pleasure
in calling one thing
by another's name?

from *American Poet*

The Opening

◇   ◇   ◇

1.

Open the door and look in.
Everything is in place.
The flicking heart
The owlet eyes are locked on.
A serpentine hair hangs over an ear.
A hand comes up to touch it.
A rhythmic hum runs ahead of the wave.
Someone turns her head
And hopes, no, lopes, across the lawn.

2.

Open the door and look in.
The magic cat is clawing the sofa.
The midnight lamp is loosing some light.
Someone is getting undressed.
Her pajamas are pressed
And she's getting into a bed of flowers.
Ophelia is lying in the bog in the park,
A moment's orphan in the afterdark.
Sing me a song, Pet, I beg of you.

3.

Open the door and look in.
The Vivian Girls are reading the books
Their countenances were cut from.
It's like a mirror. The parent and the penguin
Child. Two men with two suitcases.
The hand mirror making its lake
Last as long as it can.
The self looking the depth
Of Wallace Stevens' wife on the dime.

4.

Open the door and look in.
A murder, some mayhem, the night
News. A cloak on a hook in the closet.
There's no rug on the floor and the wood
Feels warm. There may have been an arson.
Mistakenly Released Suspect Still Missing
In Dogville or Dogtown or the Down-and-out
Sorry state of things now. Listen,
Brenda Lee is singing "I'm sorry."

5.

Open the door and look in. Look
Down the page to the footnote. To the fine print.
To the FedEx box on the bedside and
The floral print jammies that are jarring
Against the plaid previous-era paper on the wall.
Some ice-cream topper Jimmies
To top off the night. Red Yellow Blue White.
The deer-leg lamp, says Jessica, really does work—
And with that, she twirls the shade like a top.

6.

Open the door and look in.
A pin under the bed.
A dust layer on the desktop.
The minutia and microbe, the fear of failing
To ward off the inevitable, It will be done.
Whatever the It is. The static of darkness,
The dissolve of the moment.
The mouse crawls out of its house,
Remembers where it last ate a grub.

7.

Open the door, Mother, and look in.
The babies in their boxes are sleeping like beetles
In ladybug red, each with a Santa hat.
They're all at the border of risk,
All about to vanish into the past
Of the unvarnished after.
A longer word for gone. Girl.
Boy. Girl. Boy. Girl. Boy.
If we turn out the lights, they will keep.

8.

Open the door and look in.
In her pajamas, she looks thin.
Pale skin, short nails, hail on the rooftop
And window glass. January is ant dark
Every morning and early in the late afternoon.
With a gloom aspect like a seascape
That was smoke damaged above a fire grate.
The wrapped-mummy mood mutes
The emo that spins like a Catherine Wheel.

9.

Open the door and look back.
Over your shoulder. A peach-cheek
Love bird on a cage roost
Is swinging back and forth.
He's nature, but he also seems nervous.
The traffic din music comes floating in.
He's nature, but he also seems nervous.
Sing us a song, Pet, and he does. He sings of arson
In Alexandria, of Helen of Tragic of Troy.

from *Verse*

N I C K Y   B E E R

Still Life with Half-Turned Woman and Questions

◇　◇　◇

after Merwin & Hammershoi

Q. So, what are you working on these days?
　　A metaphor machine.

Q. What did you paint first?
　　A table that glints with the self-assurance of a rack.

Q. And next?
　　A bowl with the pale, rotund mien of a bureaucrat—it's the ideal
　　receptacle for a severed head.
　　Then bottles, side-by-side, like the hard parallels of a double-
　　barreled shotgun.

Q. What's that hanging on the wall, to the left of the table?
　　A mirror.
　　A window.
　　A sliding panel cut in the door of a solitary confinement cell.
　　A gray eye gone rectangular with its own blindness.

Q. No really—what's that on the wall?
　　Another picture.

Q. Why is she turned away?
　　Because she chose to wear the hex on her forehead.
　　Because she failed to gleam.
　　Because she interrupted.

Q. Why can't you sleep?
   Why can't *you* sleep?

Q. Why can't I sleep?
   Because of all these little unfacings.

from *Beloit Poetry Journal*

The Method

◇   ◇   ◇

Of the knees we might say they beseech,
seen together on the floor, the head bowed,
wherefrom one senses penitence and dread.
From a future of the numerous, a single sword
is held aloft. It takes two hands. From the sound
of no-sound the soon-to-be-beheaded is aware
the steel blade is beginning to descend. At once
the stricken neck flowers, a thousand rosettes,
and the head, picked up by its hair, dripping,
is thrown thoughtless in the trash. For an instant,
if one could be measured, the mind must resist,
while in reality time stops. Something about it.
A kind of gumshoe diplomacy kicks into action,
asking for clear pictures it dare not show.

from *Crazyhorse*

CHRISTIAN BÖK

Vowels

◇   ◇   ◇

loveless vessels

we vow
solo love

we see
love solve loss

else we see
love sow woe

selves we woo
we lose

losses we levee
we owe

we sell
loose vows

so we love
less well

so low
so level

wolves evolve

from *New American Writing*

LOUIS E. BOURGEOIS

A Voice from the City

◇   ◇   ◇

And why, Nephew, does this engine make you sad?

The night before the Communists invaded the city my uncle sat at the stone table and was transfixed by a dozen ripe bananas lying there. "Aren't they wonderful, Nephew? Isn't it wonderful that we should have such fruit in our house? We are luckier than all the kings who ruled over Cambodia—they could have all the bananas they wanted but as sated as they were, they could never eat them." My uncle was not an optimist; he had simply grown unclear in the head. He didn't sleep, he sat up all night at the stone table staring at the bananas—two days later they dragged him to the outskirts of town and shot him in the face for wearing eyeglasses.

1975

from *Sentence*

Flesh of John Brown's Flesh: Dec. 2, 1859

◇　◇　◇

We knew the rules and punishments:
three lashes for lack of diligence,
eight for disobeying mother

or telling lies. . . . *No blood,* he'd say,
and no remission. Came a day
he started keeping my account,

as at a store. And came another
he called me to the tannery:
a Sunday, day of settlement.

I'd paid one-third the owed amount
when he, to my astonishment,
handed the blue-beech switch to me.

Always, the greatest of my fears
were not his whippings, but his tears,
and he was tearful now. I dared

not disobey, nor strike him hard.
"I will consider a weak blow
no blow at all, rather a show

of cowardice," he said. *No blood
and no remission.* Thus he paid
himself the balance that I owed,

our mingled blood a token of
a thing that went unnamed: his love.
This nation, too, is his bad child,

fails him utterly, drives him wild
with rage and grief and will be scourged
nearly to death before she, purged,

may rise and stand. *No blood,* I hear
him saying still, *and no remission.*
So hang him today, Virginia; cheer

his body swaying in the air—
tomorrow you will learn what's true:
hanging's a thing he's done for you.

from *Subtropics*

Let Me Count the Ways

◇   ◇   ◇

How I miss the mountain, what it stood for,
represented, what it meant, what it said,
how it made me feel, what it did for me, that mountain,
that emergence, how it embodied the rage of whatever
it is I used to rage against, how I wanted to conquer
the mountain, scale the mountain, whether to hike it
or jog it, whether to sleep on it, whether to shoot its fauna
with camera or gun, whether to draw the mountain,
draw the view from the mountain, allude to the mountain,
name my firstborn after the mountain, before the mountain,
have a picnic at its foot, build a chairlift up it, open a tea
and sandwich shop at the end of the trail at its summit,
stamp my initials with giant concrete slabs on its face,
be the agent of the mountain, the lobbyist, the sculptor,
the detractor, sermonizer, liege, jester, or militia,
the one who unequivocally explains the mountain,
mother of the mountain, husband of the mountain, haven
for the mountain, rocking chair for the mountain,
smokejumper, clear cutter, controlled burner, doppelganger,
molehill.

from *Poet Lore*

Duties of an English Foreign Secretary

◇   ◇   ◇

Moon, refrigerate the weeping child
and guard his frozen brook.
There is no thing between the woods
like music of the band
and I've got friends in London, no I've
got friends in London,
lawyer in their hearth or billion starry heath,
in the language of mine
that they laugh at
delphiniums rev up the fire,
really look at them go
lead into the throat
a snowfield gas
a Crimean slogan,
in England
or in sum,
no papers go off bang to pad the fog.

My nation bears repeating and adores
the maudit hermit rising without name into gorgeous claimant lumber.
Here's your forest, visitor
—soft psssst of the oar—
will you hear a bird parlando
necking at your door.
That duck will float
should it be born.
My face from off its neck is torn.

I owe so much, I have no thing,
the rest I'll leave the poor.
I've seen the truth, I *have* my mind
I *have* to have that telephone,
it fit in the hand
a hundred times over
and that's not
all that's everything.
Compare this to the British isles
what I cannot describe
what I saw—
Prospero wailed on Ariel
and Ariel wailed,
"What a boom year for material!"

By the way,
all this takes place
on my lawn,
it has nothing to do with love
it is perfunctory
it is the end of the year
it is your idea and I want more of it.
Wrap my bonny hood in every paper
on the rack and please to have
a horse to cart
the grocery off my back,
now it's got late and I will go and will be back.

In the forest some hear winds adjust
a funny tuft of seed,
where is that song or stiffly-collared child
beating on a pot, but in the forest I do not,
I hear my friends are sawing in the fog.
Some hear their mouth in front
of that but face perform
the words "light company at four"
and a "mall to leaf through eye-correction
literature at eight" and couldn't that be great
I'd even trade it for a song and some hear beasts
perform an even-tempered chorus,

I only hear those friends
are sawing in the fog.

I found myself in a wood of chairs,
the birds were thin as wires,
when information fails, light falls,
the office clock to airy thinness beat.
Is it not gold to have been cheek
in front of that but guilt to bear,
take that, I live the life for the dog you eat.
Youth to fortune
instrument you are
prohibitive and lying sack of wood,
I want to walk a line
I want to play my dove
in a magic show about John Donne
but everybody does,
but everybody does
steal all the gold and silver
fall down stabbed, light a pity candle
then get up again and quote,
"I go to sleep and then get up again."

Moon, refrigerate the sitting child
and guard his frozen brook.
There is no thing between the woods
like music of the band
and I've got friends in London, no I've
got *friends* in *London*.
None of my friends reads poesie.
All around them was trees.
These friends called me sir.
I have said things I would love
to have been true, but thought
and act are crammed with chairs,
soft visitor sit down, and then?

from *Fence*

marriage

◊ ◊ ◊

On edge
and on—

whether manna or nominal
can't quite keep
a noun in the mouth.

Avid. Avidly

bare prayer came
forcing itself down
from your foot, my foot, my hand.

Formal yet mannered yet
lavished and lain

and I measure
allegiance
as leisure is rain.

from *POOL*

Common Flicker

◇　◇　◇

Old nail pounding your way
into bark or creosote,
intermittent tripod
of legs and beak,
derrick, larvae driller,

when I look up from
my mind I see what
you are: feather-hooded,
mustached, gripped
to the steady perch;

an idea of the lower
altitudes sparged
with color, a tuber
of claws and wings
and an eye unmarred.

Wing-handled hammer
packing the framer's blow,
face stropping the hardness,
drumming and drumming,
your song is your name.

This will cure me,
you declare. *This will*
heal the fractured jaw,
soothe the vibrating helve
so I can eat, so I can sing.

from *TriQuarterly*

The News Today

◇   ◇   ◇

A landslide in Bolivia,
the marriage of two chimps in a zoo in California,
snow predicted for late in the afternoon,
and on the book review page, a new translation of Catullus.

Aulelius, you cheap bastard . . .
Maximus, your ass stinks from sitting all day . . .
Pontibus, who was that plump whore you brought to
        the banquet . . . ?

Is there anyone who does not admire the forthright way
in which his poems begin
and, of course, the lively gossip that follows,
the acrid smoke of contumely
rising from the blown-out candles of the past?

No room for the daffodil here,
or the afternoon shadow of a column,
not when everyone at last night's party must be demeaned.

Who has time for sunlight falling on the city
when Capellus needs to be told he is a shitty host
and Ameana reminded that she is one horrid bitch?

Nobody does it quite like you do, Catullus,
you insulting, foulmouthed cocksucker,

and I am thrilled to hear that once again
your words have been ferried to the shores of English,
you mean-spirited pain in everyone's ass.

Without you, Catullus,
a pedestal in the drafty hall of the greats
would be missing its white marble bust.

And so I hail you, Catullus,
across the wide, open waters of literature,
you nasty motherfucker, you flaming Roman prick.

from *Bookforum*

ROBERT CREELEY

Valentine for You

◇　◇　◇

Wherefrom, whereto
the thought to do—

Wherewith, whereby
the means themselves now lie—

Wherefor, wherein
such hopes of reconciling heaven—

Even the way is changed
without you, even the day.

from *Crazyhorse*

LINH DINH

Continuous Bullets over Flattened Earth

◇   ◇   ◇

Like horizontal couriers of a vertical fate,
Like troop rotations at a service station,
Like English lessons in Guantánamo,
Like draping towels onto a bronze head,
Like spraying love onto the sand.
I went as one and came back as two.
I went as one and came back as zero.

from *New American Writing*

A Super-Clean Country

◇   ◇   ◇

You (almost) never see it in public so
You have to conjure it up all day long,
Drag it into every conversation,
To flesh out the corporate picture.

It's an inevitable verbal tic—wouldn't you say?—
For a super-clean country.

Holy shit, that shit's wack.
She thinks she's hot shit but she ain't dogshit.
There's nothing but shit on the internet.
Why are you so hung up on shit like that?
I got some good shit at home, some far-out shit.
You're so full of shit, you dumbshit motherfucker.

from *New American Writing*

MIKE DOCKINS

Dead Critics Society

◇　◇　◇

Zooks! What have I done with my anthologies? I'll need a
year of sleep after writing my millionth review (with aplomb).
XX bottles of moonshine litter my bedside table like arsenic.
Why no lilting iambics in contemporary poetry? Only dead,
vermin-ridden prose riddled with autobiographical treacle.
Under my bed, the skeleton of Browning. I use his broken-off
tibias as walking sticks. For hundreds of scenic miles I drag
sensitivity, & marvel. Content must be pounded into a rich
risotto of form—evident rhyme scheme & equal stanzas. I
quote Keats: "Gasp! I'm dying!" Were he as prosperous as J.
P. Morgan, he may not have suffered so. These days, a black-
out of good taste, a dimming of metrical etiquette, a dismal
nerve of postmodern surrealism, whatever that means. I'm
mad! I raise one of Browning's femurs in revolt! I've a notion,
ladies & gentlemen, that our language has crumbled into
kindling—a few tiny sparks, maybe, but no thick log to keep
joy in prosody truly alive. Meantime, I'm just about up to Q
in my encyclopedia of literature: Quixote, etc., but still I gather
hives hunting hopelessly for my beloved poetry anthologies.
God knows Browning would have understood—what a saint.
Five finger bones claw the floor under my bed, searching. You
entertain such a relic, you pay the price—each knuckle a shiv
digging for inspiration in the floorboards, scraping shallow
crosses into my skin as I slumber. I should lock him in a box!
But then nothing would remind me of my own bones—O my
awaiting death—the only theme suitable for a poetry buzz.

from *Atlanta Review* and *Verse Daily*

SHARON DOLIN

Tea Lay

◇　◇　◇

after John Clare

A missed tea, that piece of, to say, *Off, grief.*
We all come, by turns meretricious, to someone's wry relief.
Tangled wit, the *ought* of risible Tea Lay,
Aspiring to forswear, regretful knees sway.
I blanket or regret, fall to knees (that oldest knot):
To see—and to have been seen—and then seen not.
Eyeing behooves, else glower sense, he vents
At me for rejoining *in jaws,* summer prying.
Ear-moist, diving highest, I ease a taller thicket,
Announce Time's sick of us, foam in its spigot.
Handmaids mate in teal water (know they're not);
Handsome sires rush thither, upbraid, forged knot.
Cool delay, seeing anhedonian repast,
Too *they,* at fault, and die; lie calm, moon madder atlas.

from *New American Writing*

DENISE DUHAMEL

Language Police Report

◊　◊　◊

After Diane Ravitch's *The Language Police*

The busybody (banned as sexist, demeaning to older women) who lives next door called my daughter a tomboy (banned as sexist) when she climbed the jungle (banned; replaced with "rain forest") gym. Then she had the nerve to call her an egghead and a bookworm (both banned as offensive; replace with "intellectual") because she read fairy (banned because suggests homosexuality; replace with "elf") tales.

I'm tired of the Language Police turning a deaf ear (banned as handicapism) to my complaints. I'm no Pollyanna (banned as sexist) and will not accept any lame (banned as offensive; replace with "walks with a cane") excuses at this time.

If Alanis Morissette can play God (banned) in *Dogma* (banned as ethnocentric; replace with "Doctrine" or "Belief"), why can't my daughter play stickball (banned as regional or ethnic bias) on boy's night out (banned as sexist)? Why can't she build a snowman (banned, replace with "snow person") without that fanatic (banned as ethnocentric; replace with "believer," "follower," or "adherent") next door telling her she's going to go to hell (banned; replaced with "heck" or "darn")?

Do you really think this is what the Founding Fathers (banned as sexist; replace with "the Founders" or "the Framers") had in mind? That we can't even enjoy our Devil (banned)-ed ham sandwiches in peace? I say put a stop to this cult (banned as ethnocentric) of PC old wives' tales (banned as sexist; replace with "folk wisdom") and extremist (banned as ethnocentric; replace with "believer," "follower," or "adherent") conservative duffers (banned as demeaning to older men).

29

As an heiress (banned as sexist; replace with "heir") to the first amendment, I feel that only a heretic (use with caution when comparing religions) would try to stop American vernacular from flourishing in all its inspirational (banned as patronizing when referring to a person with disabilities) splendor.

from *Sentence*

STEPHEN DUNN

Where He Found Himself

◇   ◇   ◇

The new man unfolded a map and pointed
to a dark spot on it. "See, that's how
far away I feel all the time, right here,
among all of you," he said.
          "Yes," John the gentle mule replied,
"alienation is clearly your happiness."
But the group leader interrupted,
"Now, now, let's hear him out,
let's try to be fair." The new man felt
the familiar comfort of everyone against him.
          He went on about the stupidities
of love, life itself as one long foreclosure,
until another man said, "I was a hog,
a terrible hog, and now I'm a llama."
To which another added, "And me, I was a wolf.
Now children walk up to me, unafraid."
          The group leader asked the new man,
"What kind of animal have you been?"
"A rat that wants to remain a rat," he said,
and the group began to soften
as they remembered their own early days,
the pain before the transformation.

from *Iowa Review*

See Jack

◇   ◇   ◇

Any number of positions: See Jack asleep. See Jack up and pacing.

Any number of cups raised, emptied and lowered any number of times. See Jack drinking coffee.

Any number of brooks and fields crossed and recrossed with ever increasing accumulation. See Jack crossing and recrossing brooks and fields.

Any number of experiences repeated in ever increasing numbers of times. Any number from the perpendiculars of consciousness to the horizontals of sleep; any number.

See Jack dead, modified by an objective complement.

Where's Jane?

from *Sentence*

Etudes

◇ ◇ ◇

Autumn is a solitude.
Winter is a fortitude.
Spring is an altitude.
Summer is an attitude.

Summer is a multitude.
Autumn is an aptitude.
Winter is a Quaalude.
Spring is a prelude.

Spring is a lassitude.
Summer is a longitude.
Autumn is a gratitude.
Winter is an interlude.

Winter is a beatitude.
Spring is a platitude.
Summer is a verisimilitude.
Autumn is a semi-nude.

from *the tiny*

LANDIS EVERSON

Lemon Tree

◇   ◇   ◇

A tree that grew in the Garden of Eden
a tree of innocence called
the Tree of Good and Evil. It was harmless

as opposites are in balance. It was also
tasteless,
the taste of innocence before it is betrayed.
When God removed the wall

he gave the lemon thorns and bitterness because it had
no hostility.
It is a taste we want most to subdue. It asks
to be left alone.
We use it with fish and tea. We sugar it.

Look out the window. It stands with a donkey's
stance, hoping the day will pass.
Its scent through the curtains
cuts through
mustiness, sharp
with sweet blossoms. It hides the smell
of new babies.

from *The American Poetry Review*

Yinglish Strophes IX

◇   ◇   ◇

So ancient the way

they fight, the way
they kill themselves. She

wouldn't let you anybody
should help her. Home
she didn't. Sometimes friends

grow out you or
you grow out them.
I really don't know
her money. I'm not

raving like she does.
She likes to rave.
It's later mostly than
trees blooming. By you
is more cheap a

little. To gold let's
get. I am still
in a daisy. Who
am I gonna aggress?
It interferes with talking,
to be togetherness.

from *Barrow Street*

Daily

◇　◇　◇

Daily we match, two scrappy parlor pets
Feinting in some established glee; your tall
Coming from the dark into our hall
Commences a short bit of flirts and frets.

Our faces dangle, tags of man and wife
Tied to an apron, to a coat and hat,
Telling the cost of dowdy habits that
Tick tock the ticky tacky daytime life.

Daytime (gray time I want one hero where
I could clap bounties beaming from his eyes)
Yaps in my arms a bastard child, defies
Me while I hold it jigging in its glare.

Today I picked some ferns and buttercups
To titillate the coffee table;
But my hands shook involved in the brash babble
And all the singing yellow mouths shut up.

Today I did a washing and the line
Bowed and flopped with my job; dearly I scrubbed
To make the chirping suds fizz in the tub
And bead in bubbles. This my pudent wine.

Love, I am drunk to hiccups from my grog;
Your eyes squint freckled with much battle mud.
And when the door flies open I shall flood
My love upon the salesman or the dog.

from *Michigan Quarterly Review*

LOUISE GLÜCK

Archaic Fragment

◇   ◇   ◇

I was trying to love matter.
I taped a sign over the mirror:
You cannot hate matter and love form.

It was a beautiful day, though cold.
This was, for me, an extravagantly emotional gesture.

. . . . your poem:
tried, but could not.

I taped a sign over the first sign:
Cry, weep, thrash yourself, rend your garments—

List of things to love:
dirt, food, shells, human hair.

. . . . said
tasteless excess. Then I

rent the signs.

AIAIAIAI cried
the naked mirror.

from *Poetry*

ALBERT GOLDBARTH

Stopping by Woods on a Snowy Evening

◇　◇　◇

" . . . miles to go before I sleep," says Frost,
as if at last, at night,
the eyes shut, and the mind shuts,
and the journey halts. Of course

that's wrong. All day and into dusklight
at this flyway stop, the waterfowl
—as plump as pillows, some of them; and others
small and sleek—have settled, abob

in the wash of the river; and here,
by the hundred, they've tucked their heads
inside a wing: inside that dark
and private sky. The outward flying is done

for now, and the inward flying begins.
All one, to the odometer.

from *New Letters*

The Master

◇   ◇   ◇

Where the poet stops, the poem
begins. The poem asks only
that the poet get out of the way.

The poem empties itself
in order to fill itself up.

The poem is nearest the poet
when the poet laments
that it has vanished forever.

When the poet disappears
the poem becomes visible.

What may the poem choose,
best for the poet?
It will choose that the poet
not choose for himself.

from *The American Poetry Review*

Best Am Po

◇   ◇   ◇

The reader encountering these sections of my new long shtupfdin
"Gnostic Balloon Clings to Baboon's Neck"
may benefit from certain orientative "heads-ups."
First of all, my shtupfdins don't try to think *for* you,
they try to think *around* you, or rather, they try
to sense how we are all *being thought* by cultural constructs.
In this shtupfdin I feel I have lowered the stress index
in order to permit a valorizing of perforation
which I feel is the only platform for revisioning culture
not already under erasure from Microsoft.
As a totality, this shtupfdin concerns itself chiefly
with saturation, velocity, and sex as it might transpire
between MP3 files that embrace in the Vaseline of fictive identity.
But of course other issues enter the arena at will
and depart without warning; I think of a shtupfdin
as a kind of Penn Station of cognition.

I embrace a poetics of bewilderismo. Can we dance
while we are being digested? This is the obvious overlording issue.

The perspective in sections 3, 5, 7, 11 and 13 of "Balloon"
is that of a mermaid named Moischa. She is a junkie
who injects history into her forehead so that she can dream out
the long implosion of capitalism.
Section 8 manifests an interweaving of two discursive threads,
a thread of palinodial lust and a thread of anger-over-divorce-settlement.
From this weaving comes a *third thing*.
The reader will notice how section 15 recapitulates Heidegger's critique
of Lacan's "interior commodities" albeit in the voice of a Haitian prostitute.

There are other tips I could provide but I prefer to let the reader
"surf the intersections"—because, finally, I know nothing
except the imbricated CD-Romized overdetermination of Not Knowing.
I embrace this. And then I run to a window (aporia) and leap
before it can embrace me. Readers seeking further materials
for processing this shtupfdin can find it in its entirety on my website
disjunctotwit.com. If the editors had seen fit to publish all 28 sections
of "Gnostic Balloon Clings to Baboon's Neck" then the totality
would have been more emergent, but I am grateful to them nevertheless.
I know that somewhere someone wearing black-rimmed glasses
and showing incredible cleavage in a way both hot and intellectual
will before long take in all 28 sections and give totality of reception
to the irono-heroic shtupfdinating whirlpool that is ultimately "me."

Let me add that I long for
the rhizome of all that I have suffered
to be caramelized into a non-narrative narrative, an anti-story
that laughs bitterly in the teeth of story. Perhaps ultimately what we need
is an inversion of the very notion of progress, which points toward
my next shtupfdin "Disprog Upchuck" which is forthcoming hyper-soon.

from *POOL*

Initiation

◇　◇　◇

After I stumbled through the gauntlet, after they had hit me
As hard as they could,
Some there only because there was somebody else
To be brought in, I joined them
In greeting the new ones, the frightened and longing ones,
And I punched as hard and as much as I could, something
Filling in me I would tell you was a thrill
Only because I had no better word for it.
There was another word for it: violence
Made my mother impatient with me, she would call me evil,
And I knew what she was trying to talk to me about—
How much I hated,
How much I wanted and how greedy wanting made me.
What I wanted most were better words.

from *The American Poetry Review*

From "The Future of Terror/Terror of the Future" Series

◇ ◇ ◇

THE FUTURE OF TERROR / 7

From the gable window, we shot
at what was left: gargoyles and garden gnomes.
I accidentally shot the generator
which would have been hard to gloss over
in a report except we weren't writing reports
anymore. We ate our gruel and watched
the hail crush the hay we'd hoped to harvest.
I found a handkerchief drying on a hook
and without a hint of irony, pocketed it.
Here was my hypothesis: we were inextricably
fucked. We'd killed all the inventors and all
the jesters just when we most needed humor
and invention. The lake breeze was lugubrious
at best, couldn't lift the leaves. As the day
lengthened, we knew we'd reached the lattermost
moment. The airlift wasn't on its way. Make-believe
was all I had left but I couldn't help but see
there was no "we"—you were a mannequin
and I'd been flying solo. I thought about how birds
can turn around mid-air. About how
the nudibranch has no notion it might need
a shell. Swell. I ate the last napoleon—

it said *Onward!* on the packaging. There was one
shot left in my rifle. So this is how you live
in the present. I polish my plimsolls.
I wrap myself in a quilt. I re-ink
my note (for nobody) and I'm ready.

Terror of the Future / 7

Sweetheart, there's no one on the street.
I attached the speakers to the steeple
but even on its loudest setting, the stereo
gets no reaction. If you ask me, (ask me,
please) the split screen of the brain
needs a sounding board, doesn't like the only
signals in the skyway to be its own synapses,
doesn't want to go solo in the sandbox.
You're. Not. Breathing. Let's see: memories.
I remember the rocking chair that was always
in the repair shop for liking to rock backward
but not forward. I remember the price
of a pressurized suit. I remember the red ribbon
in your hair. I remember when pandemonium
was possible. O there's no way to nectarize this moment—
it's entirely without sweetness. In just a minute
it'll be match point and of course the world wins.
It's not a matter of life-and-death, it's life or
death. Here in the grove, after jar after jar
of grain alcohol, the sun looks like a halo,
then a noose. Give me a helping hand,
historian. Help me with that "or."

from *BOMB*

Bush's War

◇　◇　◇

I typed the brief phrase, "Bush's War,"
At the top of a sheet of white paper,
Having some dim intuition of a poem
Made luminous by reason that would,
Though I did not have them at hand,
Set the facts out in an orderly way.
Berlin is a northerly city. In May
At the end of the twentieth century
In the leafy precincts of Dahlem Dorf,
South of the Grunewald, near Krumme Lanke,
Spring is northerly; it begins before dawn
In a racket of bird song. The *amsels*
Shiver the sun up as if they were shaking
A liquid tangle of golden wire. There are two kinds
Of flowering chestnuts, red and white,
And the wet pavements are speckled
With petals from the incandescent spikes
Of their flowers and shoes at U-bahn stops
Are flecked with them. Green of holm oaks,
Birch tassels, the soft green of maples,
And the odor of lilacs is everywhere.
At Oskar Helene Heim station a farmer
Sells white asparagus from a heaped table.
In a month he'll be selling chanterelles;
In the month after that, strawberries
And small, rosy crawfish from the Spree.
The piles of stalks of the asparagus
Are startlingly phallic, phallic and tender
And deathly pale. Their seasonal appearance

Must be the remnant of some fertility ritual
Of the German tribes. Steamed, they are the color
Of old ivory. In May, in restaurants
They are served on heaped white platters
With boiled potatoes and parsley butter,
Or shavings of Parma ham and lemon juice
Or sorrel and smoked salmon. And,
Walking home in the slant, widening,
Brilliant northern light that falls
On the new-leaved birches and the elms,
Nightingales singing at the first, subtlest,
Darkening of dusk, it is a trick of the mind
That the past seems just ahead of us,
As if we were being shunted there
In the surge of a rattling funicular.
Flash forward: the firebombing of Hamburg,
Fifty thousand dead in a single night,
"The children's bodies the next day
Set in the street in rows like a market
In charred chicken." Flash forward:
Firebombing of Tokyo, a hundred thousand
In a night. Flash forward: forty-five
Thousand Polish officers slaughtered
By the Russian army in the Katyn Woods,
The work of half a day. Flash forward:
Two million Russian prisoners of war
Murdered by the German army all across
The eastern front, supplies low,
Winter of 1943. Flash: Hiroshima.
And then Nagasaki, as if the sentence
Life is fire and flesh is ash needed
To be spoken twice. Flash: Auschwitz,
Dachau, Theriesenstadt, the train lurching,
The stomach woozy, past displays of falls
Of hair, piles of valises, spectacles
With frames designed to curl delicately
Around a human ear. Flash:
The gulags, seven million in Byelorussia
And Ukraine. In innocent Europe on a night
In spring, among the light-struck birches,

Students holding hands. One of them
Is carrying a novel, the German translation
Of a slim book by Marguerite Duras
About a love affair in old Saigon. (Flash:
Two million Vietnamese, fifty-five thousand
Of the American young, whole races
Of tropical birds extinct from saturation bombing)
The kind of book the young love
To love, about love in time of war.
Forty-five million, all told, in World War II.
In Berlin, pretty Berlin, in the spring time,
You are never not wondering how
It happened, and the people around you
In the station with chestnut petals on their shoes,
Children then, or unborn, never not
Wondering. Is it that we like the kissing
And bombing together, in prospect
At least, girls in their flowery dresses?
Someone will always want to mobilize
Death on a massive scale for economic
Domination or revenge. And the task, taken
As a task, appeals to the imagination.
The military is an engineering profession.
Look at boys playing: they love
To figure out the ways to blow things up.
But the rest of us have to go along.
Why do we do it? Certainly there's a rage
To injure what's injured us. Wars
Are always pitched to us that way.
The well-paid news readers read the reasons
On the air. And we who are injured,
Or have been convinced that we are injured,
Are always identified with virtue. It's that—
The rage to hurt mixed with self-righteousness
And fear—that's murderous.
The young Arab depilated himself
As an act of purification before he drove
The plane into the office building. It's not
Just violence, it's a taste for power
That amounts to loathing for the body.

Perhaps it's this that permits people to believe
That the dead women in the rubble of Baghdad
Who did not cast a vote for their deaths
Or the glimpse afforded them before they died
Of the raw white of the splintered bones
In the bodies of their men or their children
Are being given the gift of freedom
Which is the virtue of their injured killers.
It's hard to say which is worse about this,
The moral sloth of it or the intellectual disgrace.
And what good are our judgments to the dead?
And death the cleanser, Walt Whitman's
Sweet death, the scourer, the tender
Lover, shutter of eyelids, turns
The heaped bodies into summer fruit,
Magpies eating dark berries in the dusk
And birch pollen staining sidewalks
To the faintest gold. *Bald nur*—Goethe—no,
Warte nur, bald ruhest du auch. Just wait.
You will be quiet soon enough. In Dahlem,
Under the chestnuts, in the leafy spring.

from *The American Poetry Review*

Critique of Pure Reason

◇　◇　◇

"Like one man milking a billy goat,
another holding a sieve beneath it,"
Kant wrote, quoting an unnamed ancient.
It takes a moment to notice the sieve doesn't matter.
In her nineties, a woman begins to sleepwalk.
One morning finding pudding and a washed pot,
another the opened drawers of her late husband's dresser.
After a while, anything becomes familiar,
though the Yiddish jokes of Auschwitz
stumbled and failed outside the barbed wire.
Perimeter is not meaning, but it changes meaning,
as wit increases distance and compassion erodes it.
Let reason flow like water around a stone, the stone remains.
A dog catching a tennis ball lobbed into darkness
holds her breath silent, to keep the descent in her ears.
The goat stands patient for two millennia,
watching without judgment from behind his strange eyes.

from *Ploughshares*

DANIEL JOHNSON

Do Unto Others

◊　◊　◊

How many rocks would I stack
on my brother's chest? A rock
for his beauty, a rock for his trust,

and two for lips redder
than a boy's should be.
Granite for his love

of birds; a chunk of quartz
shot through with pink.
For singing on car trips,

hiding in the dryer, and flouncing
down Oak Street in my mother's dress:
limestone, shale, sandstone, flint,

limestone, shale, sandstone, flint.

from *Barrow Street*

51

Auguries

◇　◇　◇

1. GODS WROUGHT

And another thing, Professor: if Heaven is
A field generated by neurology,
And gods are seen as knots or local disturbances

Of the field, doesn't the sheer evanescence
Of it horrify first? Wouldn't raw logic
Require it all to flicker, should the turbines

Fail and whirr down? *Then wink out?* The nonsense
Verse and husky stonepiles of Religion
All that's left, their casketry—The gods, on pins

And needles, must suspect this. Excitation in the xenon
Tube! Wave functions collapsing throughout the Elysian
Field! Noses pressed to the police-glass of penance:

Insentient they may be; that doesn't make them stupid.
Gods must watch augurs slit live birds, too.

2. AUGUR GONE

But what if our augurs, scratching at the new,
Whatever that is, should watch by auspices
Some bird-speck up the sweep of the long blue
Resolve again into a *god?*—waspish,

Close-clung, driving the filed spurs
Of his intention home into the future
Through the tissue of the breast?—To pierce
The veil of the real again!—that would be virtue

In its root sense. No flickery hologram,
But Man, knee deep in the magma pool of dawn
Again, bleeding out imaginary grammars
Hot enough to speak what eidolons

We dream: gods again, not numbers numbing
Heaven to a thought, but *real gods* again, or coming.

from *Southwest Review*

Comma of God

◇ ◇ ◇

I am nothing compared to the Medicaid sneer
I am nothing compared to the owner of the door
I am nothing compared to the elevator of Heidegger
I am nothing compared to the spokes of Vincent's Belgian sunflower
I am nothing compared to Rodin's least mistress
I am nothing compared to the frames of Hamlet
I am nothing compared to a critic or chauffeur
I am nothing compared to my old fire engine
I am nothing compared to the breasts I see
I am nothing compared to a tree in any season
I am nothing compared to the escalator of Duchamp
I am nothing compared to Marinetti's future
I am nothing to compare with Turner's clouds
I am nothing to compare with the lens of Claude
I am nothing to compare with my mother in 1930
I am nothing to compare with the cockroach in the drain
I am nothing to compare to the jew-hater's snot
I am nothing compared to the beak or the bill
I am nothing compared to the past or the present
I am nothing to compare with any suit on the rack
I am nothing to compare to a loaf or child
I am nothing to compare with any syllable of Homer
I am nothing to compare with the foot of a chair
I am nothing to compare with the truth of your anger
I am nothing compared with what I failed to do
I am nothing compared with one note of Lester Young
I am nothing compared to the images of Vietnam
I am nothing compared to the furnace of Dresden

I am nothing compared to the last drops of snow
I am nothing compared to a bicycle with wings
I am nothing compared to the comma of God

from *Sentence*

GALWAY KINNELL

Hide-and-Seek, 1933

◇   ◇   ◇

Once when we were playing
hide-and-seek and it was time
to go home, the rest gave up
on the game before it was done
and forgot I was still hiding.
I remained hidden as a matter
of honor until the moon rose.

from *Beloit Poetry Journal*

Ode to the Personals

◇ ◇ ◇

Reading the English-language classifieds, Florence, Fall 2004

She says she is 170 centimeters, which sounds like
a lot of centimeters, though it probably isn't.
    But what's the meaning of "with just 33 years already
        for several years executing and influencing worldwide
very important missions"? If she's saying she's 33, okay,
    but if she's been traveling the world for 33 years,
        unless she started when she was a toddler,

    she must have a lot of centimeters on her odometer, so to speak.
And her "missions" involve "executing," which,
    you'll agree, is a hell of a way of "influencing" somebody.
        One ad down, a competitor describes herself simply
as "Lone lady, 53." Yeah, like "lone wolf."
    Scientists say all women lie about age and weight,
        all men about height and marital status.

One romantic seeks someone who "possesses integrity,
is affluent, well-educated, and marriage-minded,"
    though if they're really affluent, I wouldn't count on them
        being overendowed in the integrity department.
And most want to "share their life and start a family," which to me
    means all these cousins showing up later,
        ignorant, impecunious narcissists whose sole subject

of conversation is themselves. One woman wants
a "Caucasian, athletic man of depth, humor and intellect
    between the ages of 43 and 50, who is open to new ideas

and adventures and available for travel to the U.S.,"
though it sounds as though his first stop will be the ATM:
Okay, Whitey, empty that account, because Emma Lazarus
is waiting for us, knife in one hand,

gun in the other. If you can't tell how tall a woman is,
how can you know the contents of her heart? A woman
might vow one thing to you and mean
quite another, might promise total sexual fidelity
and then reveal that she meant she'd only be faithful to you on the feasts
of San Valentino and the nativity of the Madonna
as well as alternate weekends, for love

is a hotchpotch, as screwy a deal as Guglielmo
Marconi's original telephone, on display at the Palazzo Strozzi
in this very city even as I write this poem
and no beautiful Bakelite affair with gold-trimmed dial
and handset, either, but a decidedly after-market cigar box
bristling with wires and knobs yet into which enters
and from which spews every note in love's long aria,

all the divers billings and cooings, the crab-assings,
the lies outright and subtle, the protestations
of love pyrotechnic, perfunctory, and Vulcan—
I say pick that phone up, reader, and call the woman
who is "thoroughly impressed by humanitarian values
and loves animals, antiques, ballet" and invite her
for coffee and a custard tart at Patrizio Così in Florence

or a coffee and strudel *mit Schlag* at Bazar in Salzburg
or tea and a big chocolate meringue cookie at Ladurée in Paris,
and she accepts! She accepts! Then it's risotto with white truffles
at Dal Pescatore outside Mantova and *Wiener Schnitzel*
at Steirereck in Vienna and warm goat cheese on *frisée*
at Le Pré aux Clercs in Dijon followed by backpacking
in the Cinque Terre and hang-gliding at Interlochen

and windsurfing at Les Sables d'Olonne
and ballroom dancing in Bern and Baltimore and Bangkok—
any kind of dancing, really, as long as it's to an upbeat

tempo so the adept can do the merengue,
the less adept the twist, and the totally spazzed-out the hokey pokey!
Not to mention natation and equitation and prestidigitation
and slipping down back canals in gondolas and junks

and feluccas and caravels and catamarans and canoes,
and the next thing you know, you're married, and she's throwing
her legs all over the place as the ocelots
and greyhounds mewl and bark and topple
the armoire and chifforobe. And if she turns out
to be 170 meters or 170 millimeters, so much the better:
that way she can carry you around or you her.

from *Five Points*

What Bee Did

◊   ◊   ◊

Bee not only buzzed.
When swatted at, Bee deviled,
Bee smirched. And when fuddled,
like many of us, Bee labored, Bee reaved.
He behaved as well as any Bee can have.

Bee never lied. Bee never lated.
And despite the fact Bee took, Bee also stowed.
In love, Bee sieged. Bee seeched.
Bee moaned, Bee sighed himself,
Bee gat with his Beloved.

And because Bee tokened summer
(the one season we all, like Bee, must lieve)
Bee also dazzled.

from *The Cortland Review*

A Good List

◇   ◇   ◇

hommage to Lorenz Hart

Some nights, can't sleep, I draw up a list,
  Of everything I've never done wrong.
To look at me now, you might insist
  My list could hardly be long,
But I've stolen no gnomes from my neighbor's yard,
Or struck his dog, backing out my car.
Never ate my way up and down the Loire
  On a stranger's credit card.

I've never given a cop the slip,
  Stuffed stiffs in a gravel quarry,
Or silenced Cub Scouts on a first camping trip
  With an unspeakable ghost story.
Never lifted a vase from a museum foyer,
Or rifled a Turkish tourist's backpack.
Never cheated at golf. Or slipped out a blackjack
  And flattened a patent lawyer.

I never forged a lottery ticket,
  Took three on a two-for-one pass,
Or, as a child, toasted a cricket
  With a magnifying glass.
I never said "air" to mean "err," or obstructed
Justice, or defrauded a securities firm.
Never mulcted—so far as I understand the term.
  Or unjustly usufructed.

I never swindled a widow of all her stuff
    By means of a false deed and title
Or stood up and shouted, *My God, that's enough!*
    At a nephew's piano recital.
Never practiced arson, even as a prank,
Brightened church-suppers with off-color jokes,
Concocted an archeological hoax—
    Or dumped bleach in a goldfish tank.

Never smoked opium. Or smuggled gold
    Across the Panamanian Isthmus.
Never hauled back and knocked a rival out cold,
    Or missed a family Christmas.
Never borrowed a book I *intended* to keep.
. . . My list, once started, continues to grow,
Which is all for the good, but just goes to show
    It's the good who do not sleep.

from *The New Criterion*

BEN LERNER

From Angle of Yaw

◇　◇　◇

HE HAD ENOUGH RESPECT FOR PAINTING to quit. Enough respect for quitting to paint. Enough respect for the figure to abstract. For abstraction to hint at the breast. For the breast to ask the model to leave. But I live here, says the model. And I respect that, says the painter. But I have enough respect for respect to insist. For insistence to turn the other cheek. For the other cheek to turn the other cheek. Hence I appear to be shaking my head *No*.

★　　　★　　　★

THE AIRCRAFT ROTATES about its longitudinal axis, shifting the equinoxes slowly west. Our system of measure is anchored by the apparent daily motion of stars that no longer exist. When the reader comes to, the writer hits him again. Just in case God isn't dead, our astronauts carry side arms. This is not your captain speaking, thinks the captain. A magnetic field reversal turns our fire friendly. Fleeing populations leave their bread unleavened, their lines unbroken.

from *Beloit Poetry Journal*

JOANIE MACKOWSKI

When I was a dinosaur

◇　◇　◇

I was stegosaurus, a.k.a. "armed roof lizard," with seventeen
headstones growing from my spine. And not one brain

but two: the first, a walnut wedged in my skull;
the other a brick at the root of my sex. I wasn't whole.

And I thought I was a seed pod, that some beak
might crack my husk and make my roots take

root: to be a bloom like a sweet pea, purple
and drunk to smell. I didn't foresee the rubble

and the ice, the ages of seep and budge,
the wonder of photosynthesis and each

new life. I love the orchids best, every bulbous god
they pull from their spines, but I see nothing good

about people. No ceiling arcs
from the bones of their backs,

and each of their brains sprouts a long gray tooth:
to think of the sun, they bite it in half.

from *POOL*

By Accident

◇　◇　◇

First she gave me the wound by accident.
Then the tourniquet she tied unwound by accident.

Your friend may want to start running.
I gave his scent to the hounds by accident.

Balloons on the mailbox, ambulance in the driveway.
Bobbing for apples I drowned by accident.

Did someone tell the devil we were building Eden?
Or did he slither on the grounds by accident?

I said some crazy things, but I swear, officer,
I burned her place down by accident.

Only surfaces interest me.
What depths I sound I sound by accident.

"What should we look for in a ghazal, Amit?"
Inevitabilities found by accident.

from *The Antioch Review*

The 10 Stages of Beatrice

◇   ◇   ◇

Stage 1.—Belonging.

In the first stage Beatrice is precisely labeled and timed. She is able to devise complex graphs, answer questions in the order that they're asked, and construct coherent narratives without nostalgia or actual fear. There is no display of loud sobbing, nor are there visions.

Stage 2.—Happy.

Beatrice, during the second stage, believes she is alive. The possibility that she is not alive, in this stage, never enters her mind. This stage is only possible if the spectacle comes to town.

Stage 3.—Walter B.

This stage is also called "the latch stage." It is Beatrice at her most historical and strange.

Stage 4.—Romance.

Beatrice is hunted, captured, and softly strung to a tree. In this stage words are used to intoxicate, supply, and deceive. These words are rarely interesting. Gifts are exchanged that are of no use.

Stage 5.—Dread.

Beatrice is covered in feathers and twigs. She believes she is a nest. This stage, if it occurs in winter, is also called "The Babies."

Stage 6.—Slice.

The sixth stage often appears in Beatrice's hand like a long instrument with a blade at the end. She will eat cake, during this stage, until she has visions.

Stage 7.—Cryptozoology.

In the seventh stage Beatrice wears a green dress with large white pockets in which to store the evidence. If this stage is mingled with the second stage, ecstasy is achieved.

Stage 8.—Crowded.

Beatrice is behind glass. In this stage Beatrice is blurred by the humans who observe her without caution.

Stage 9.—Poland.

Beatrice gathers her grandfather into her arms. She recites him from his memory. The ninth stage sounds like this: *tsim tsum, tsim tsum, tsim tsum.*

Stage 10.—Return.

In the final stage Beatrice watches Beatrice feed the babies with a spade.

from *Conduit*

Ode to the Plantar Fascia

◇   ◇   ◇

Latin cousin to Achilles,
architectural upholder
bearing its magisterial bundle
beneath an imperial arch,
rods around axe
around
axle and axis,
staunch stanchion of the canonical self,
aquiline and august,
tensile, earthly, planted
and wound in sinewed plaits,

inverted hammock
on which the body rests its burden
like a red-faced tourist
in the shadow
of a coconut palm,

only now is your grievance
made known to me,
and my dignity is hobbled,

only now do I hear your cry,
unenviable membrane,
faithful attendant upon my every stride,
tender sole, antipodal to the soul,
pale mirror to the palm
of this hand,

only now do I honor your service,
only now do I learn to address you by name,

and the Empire
trembles.

from *POOL*

On Leonardo's Drawings

◇　◇　◇

AIM

The palaeolithic bowman well knew where to find the heart
of his victim, and he has portrayed it transfixed with arrows
on the walls of his shelter.
　　　　　—Charles Singer's account of the Western world's
　　　　　　earliest anatomists, *A Short History of Anatomy*

Elmer Belt says Leonardo's drawings of the genital tracts
somehow failed to find their way with all the rest
to Windsor Castle's collection of the Queen.
These scrolls and doodles worked their way instead
to Weimar's *Schlossmuseum,* the German royals
making slightly less to-do over maps of genitalia
than the Brits, but Elmer doesn't care to reproduce
Leonardo's most offensive image, man and woman
joined in coitus, their hips and thighs transparent,
so the penis gaining entry can be seen in its entirety,
their entrails coiled like vines of acorn squash,
while his substantial shaft aims for the open mouth
of her barracuda uterus. Though she has no bones
besides her half a spine, Leonardo's taken care to sketch
her lover's open eye tipped toward the empty space
of her missing face, which I imagine must, like Bernini's
naughty Saint Teresa, tip backward, eyes entirely closed
in legal ecstasy as the arrow points where we all know
God won't go. But Leonardo's man exudes a proper diffidence,
ample bonnet of curls whispering down the elegant

swirl of his tail as he throws one High Renaissance leg
over the mere suggestion of her thigh
and aims his animal spirit in.

WANDERING UTERUS

Leonardo believed that semen came down
from the brain through a channel in the spine.

And that female lactation held its kick off
in the uterus. Not as bad as Hippocrates

who thought the womb wandered the ruddy
crags of a woman's body, wreaking a havoc

whenever it lodged, shoving aside
more sensible organs like the heart.

All manner of moral failings, snits
and panics were thus explained, the wayward

organ floating like Cleopatra's barge
down the murky canal of any appendage

or tying up at the bog of the throat.
One can't help but imagine a little halved

walnut of a boat like that in Leonardo's
drawing, the curled meat of the fetus

tucked inside, harboring near a naughty eye
or rebellious ear that never can hear

what a man might mean when he says *yes*
or *always*. It's all still beautifully true

what these good scientists alleged: the brain
is as good a place as any for the manufacture

of evanescence, and why not allow
that the round and sturdy skiff of the uterus

may float and flaunt its special appetite for novelty,
even if we dub it dumb, lined with tentacles,

many chambered, and errant as the proverbial knight
seeking out adventure, but loyal to one queen.

from *The Kenyon Review*

Etymology

◊   ◊   ◊

The filth hissed at us when we venture out—
always in twos or threes, never alone—
seems less a language *spoken* than one *spat*
in savage plosives, primitive, obscene:
a cavemob nya-nya, limited in frame
of reference and novelty, the same
suggestions of what we or they could do,
or should, *ad infinitum.* Yesterday
a mill girl spat a phrase I'd never heard
before. I stopped and looked at her, perplexed.
I derived its general meaning from the context,
but was stumped by the etymology of one word.
What was its source? Which demon should we thank
for words it must be an abomination to think?

from *Literary Imagination*

Voltaire at Cirey, 1736

◇ ◇ ◇

Emilie, the love of his life,
took him to her castle
where they built laboratories
and libraries and workrooms
for the life of the mind
as well as the bed
and studied Newton
and Locke and recruited neighbors
to act in plays and read poetry
aloud at 4 A.M. and enjoyed
"exquisite food and wine"
and such were the times
that even Emilie's husband
became fond of Voltaire
and once, catching the great man
with another woman, scolded him
for being "unfaithful to us."

Perhaps this is what the phrase
"the Enlightenment" means,
though their behavior titillated
most of France which acted like us
reading *People* and *Star*
clucking, sanctimonious and jealous—
slaves to our sadnesses, envious—

though of course we'd draw a blank
at the Newton and the Locke
and the poetry parts.

from *Barrow Street*

Peep Show

◇   ◇   ◇

Tokens in the slot:
ka-shot, shot, shot.
A figure in the darkness.
The tin crank
of canned do-wop.

Someone is always watching—
don't you think?
Duck, turn, and wink.
Bodies at a distance—
that's what we are,

raises, renovations, Florida,
dinner by the sea.
Look at you.
The waves go swiftly
out of sight—

a long ellipsis
of glaciers swallowing the sun—
come quick, no time for this,
the girls in thongs
are glancing at the clock.

from *The Kenyon Review*

GREGORY ORR

From Concerning the Book That Is the Body of the Beloved

◊   ◊   ◊

Weeping, weeping, weeping.
No wonder the oceans are full;
No wonder the seas are rising.

It's not the beloved's fault.
Dying is part of the story.
It's not your fault either:
Tears are also.
                     But
You can't read when you're
Crying. Sobbing, you won't
Hear the song that resurrects
The body of the beloved.

Why not rest a while? If weeping
Is one of the world's tasks,
It doesn't lack adherents.
Someone will take your place,
Someone will weep for you.

from *Rattle*

77

Dear Pearce & Pearce, Inc.

◇　◇　◇

I trail your feathered leavings. I see around the ground-level,
cracked half-panes where you've been tramping. A bitty crescent
told off by a length of slit hose, where the leaves molder, and
what you leave molders. A sparkplug.

Tell me, said Zorba, do he & he make you feel for your temperature?
Do he & he have a muscle big in the arm from the aiming? Do he
& he pay for it when you dine at the surgeon's? And I say.

Every time. Here is my wallet, my truncated prescription.
Purse your lips. A regatta of providers ensues.

from *Denver Quarterly*

A Tech's Ode to the Genome Computer

◇　◇　◇

Charming, how you hammer
human glamour and the hymn everything sings

to everything into
one. Honey, what your bubble jets dissect

into text. What your haters want:
facelift of the wrinkled scrolls

pulsing on old temple walls.
What you spit: nude

truth. Smoothing a wet billionth
of it into a mist of ink, I'm

moved. I like the shine, dry, die
of that light in my fingerprints.

Won't insult you with bone-deep
phobias—genetics' liquid skeletons spilling

into flight, staining
sky brain-gray. You won't refuel the old school

cartridge of my recurring nightmare—
one tech's blood in your printer,

veins of yours truly turned black as syn-
tax, and you, silicone madonna,

reaching for the feed of my paper heart
for the only code

I need you so
never to read.

from *The Kenyon Review*

SUSAN PARR

Swooping Actuarial Fauna

◊   ◊   ◊

They blow downwind.
Quivering bulletins,
Details in a coil,
A many-thing,
Chosen by by-paths,
Shadows falling
To statistical stalls—
Whistling wherewithals.

from *Alaska Quarterly Review*

SUSAN PARR

Ecstatic Cling

◇   ◇   ◇

You will singe your arm when you pluck him from the air.
—Susan Stewart

Bitten by the electrician's boy—
my shoulder drizzled in his spit, my soul
a porcupine—I stuck one little thumb
into his cheek (to get inside the den, to grab
the guilty tooth). He clobbered me. *Oh* and *Ow*
and *No* around the room—I fought with the son
until he charged into a static hug; we spun
as coupling cats become, too caught for giving up.
He lost his tooth; his tongue kept re-erupting
through the hole—against my neck I felt the nose
of something small and living, a wetter pocking
than my sweat against his shirt snaps. I fastened
to him, we burned against the rug until I dropped.
It hurt to hold the boy—though he was light enough.

from *Alaska Quarterly Review*

Nursemaid's Elbow

◇　◇　◇

—a partial dislocation of the elbow, caused
by a sudden pull on a child's arm or hand.
                                        For K.F.

Named not for the mother, frazzled and rushed,
nor for the toddler who knows just when to flop.

Not for the swinging up from her tantrum,
nor for how swiftly it happens, the soft

chicken-wing pop. Not for the child
silent in ER, unable to lift

her left arm, nor for the X-ray showing
her radius slipped from its usual spot.

Not for the doctor cupping her elbow,
turning her palm back and up. Not for his thumb

finessing the ligament, nor for how
soon she's playing again with her dolls. But

for this: stern servant, hired helpstress, easy
scapegoat—the one who was not even there.

from *New England Review*

Louie Louie

⋄   ⋄   ⋄

I have heard of Black Irish but I never
Heard of White Catholic or White Jew.
I have heard of "Is Poetry Popular?" but I
Never heard of Lawrence Welk Drove
Sid Caesar Off Television.

I have heard of Kwanzaa but I have
Never heard of Bert Williams.
I have never heard of Will
Rogers or Roger Williams
Or Buck Rogers or Pearl Buck
Or Frank Buck or Frank
Merriwell At Yale.

I had heard of Yale but I never
Heard of George W. Bush.
I have heard of Harvard but I
Never heard of Numerus Clausus
Which sounds to me like
Some kind of Pig Latin.

I have heard of the Pig Boy.

I have never heard of the Beastie
Boys or the Scottsboro Boys but I
Have heard singing Boys, what
They were called I forget.

I have never heard America
Singing but I have heard of I
Hear America Singing, I think
It must have been a book
We had in school, I forget.

from *The American Poetry Review*

Stupid Meditation on Peace

◇   ◇   ◇

"He does not come to coo."
—Gerard Manley Hopkins

Insomniac monkey-mind ponders the Dove,
Symbol not only of Peace but sexual
Love, the couple nestled and brooding.

After coupling, the human animal needs
The woman safe for nine months and more.
But the man after his turbulent minute or two

Is expendable. Usefully rash, reckless
For defense, in his void of redundancy
Willing to death and destruction.

Monkey-mind envies the male Dove
Who equally with the female secretes
Pigeon-milk for the young from his throat.

For peace, send all human males between
Fourteen and twenty-five to school
On the Moon, or better yet Mars.

But women too are capable of Unpeace,
Yes, and we older men too, venom-throats.
Here's a great comic who says on our journey

We choose one of two tributaries: the River
Of Peace, or the River of Productivity.
The current of Art he says runs not between

Banks with birdsong in the fragrant shadows—
No, an artist must follow the stinks and rapids
Of the branch that drives millstones and dynamos.

Is peace merely a vacuum, the negative
Of creation, or the absence of war?
The teaching says Peace is a positive energy.

Still something in me resists that sweet milk,
My mind resembles my restless, inferior cousin
Who fires his shit in handfuls from his cage.

from *The New Yorker*

The Rev. Larry Love Is Dead

◇　◇　◇

He's dead now,

his balls will
never get itchy
again—
　　　　because he's dead now forever—

his hair having been
hennaed free of charge
for one last time
by the Egyptian cosmetologists
at the Style Connection,
　　　　　　　　there's no doubt now that he's dead—

Thanks to a fury
in his bloodhall,

he's good & gone forever.

The sun tho
is bright today,
　　　　　　a constancy, a slivered glinting in the airstream—

and, musically-speaking,
the bluejay
swinging amid our pines has got himself

a permanent hard-on
it seems—
        on the radio next door
the tunes of another era,
              still very much without error,

the Everlys,
the miscreant pheromone
Sly Stone, Barry White
of the undulant jherricurls,

and every 6th or 7th song
the always early-autumn river foam
of tenor Orbison—

        why is it the world gets in his way like this?

      from *TriQuarterly*

MARYA ROSENBERG

"If I Tell You You're Beautiful, Will You Report Me?": A West Point Haiku Series

◇   ◇   ◇

the delicate pinkish
late-afternoon light shines through
the bullet holes.

Romance at West Point—"If
I tell you you're beautiful,
will you report me?"

under her muddy
battle-dress uniform—an
orange push-up bra

a small blonde cadet
girl sleeps peacefully in her
"Death from Above" shirt

crewcut teenager
with rows of medals—a colonel
in the JROTC

A Frequently Asked Question:
"Why does the eternal light in the chapel
appear to be unlit?"

"Do Not Mess With The Bat.
The Officer-In-Charge Will
Take Care of It."

The National Anthem plays—
the Army mule refuses
to stand at attention

shirtless lacrosse team—
a blue-eyed girl tells the bus driver
to slow down

Springtime at West Point
boys in combat boots, slipping
on cherry blossoms.

Cadet romance—"Want
to check *me* for ticks?" she asks
him flirtatiously

first kiss—hiding
behind the memorial to the
Bataan Death March

martial arts class—he
twists my arm backwards to
kiss the inside of my wrist

We slept in the trash
heap, and I lay all night warm
in his arms.

The yellow leaf looks
briefly like a butterfly
as it falls.

On our ancient gray
stone walls, the poison ivy
ripples in the breeze

In the spider's cage,
the crickets are singing.

from *Hanging Loose*

F

◇   ◇   ◇

Firethorn: a trope for
Fucking, which people talk entirely too much about, the
Flurry of phonemes a substitute,
Foucault would say. I'm beginning to be
Free of it. Reading
Feldenkrais makes me blush, how much it mattered. I'd rather swim than
Fornicate. Laura asks, how often? It depends what you mean by sex, I say. I never
Fetishized, was never caught in
Flagrante delicto.
Forget the times I'd pull to the side of the road
For some, heating up at 30
Fahrenheit outside. It's a
Falcon honing in on a nest of mice, a venomous
Fang, a
Farce in Braille and Esperanto. And
Freud, was he ever wrong! About inversion, envy, and hysteria. O
Faucet I've turned to a trickle, O
Fracas muffled in silk, I don't give a
Fig—your furor and fuss have
passed, o bittersweet.

from *Beloit Poetry Journal*

The Death of the Shah

◇　◇　◇

Here I am, not a practical man,
But clear-eyed in my contact lenses,
Following no doubt a slightly different line than the others,
Seeking sexual pleasure above all else,
Despairing of art and of life,
Seeking protection from death by seeking it
On a racebike, finding release and belief on two wheels,
Having read a book or two,
Having eaten well,
Having traveled not everywhere in sixty-seven years but far,
Up the Eiffel Tower and the Leaning Tower of Pisa
And the World Trade Center Twin Towers
Before they fell,
Mexico City, Kuala Lumpur, Accra,
Tokyo, Berlin, Teheran under the Shah,
Cairo, Bombay, L.A., London,
Into the jungles and the deserts and the cities on the rivers
Scouting locations for the movie,
A blue-eyed white man with brown hair,
Here I am, a worldly man,
Looking around the room.

Any foal in the kingdom
The Shah of Iran wanted
He had brought to him in a military helicopter
To the palace.
This one was the daughter of one of his ministers, all legs, a goddess.
She waited in a room.
It was in the afternoon.

I remember mounds of caviar before dinner
In a magnificent torchlit tent,
An old woman's beautiful house, a princess,
Three footmen for every guest,
And a man who pretended to get falling-down drunk
And began denouncing the Shah,
And everyone knew was a spy for the Shah.

A team of New York doctors (mine among them)
Was flown to Mexico City to consult.
They were not allowed to examine the Shah.
They could ask him how he felt.

The future of psychoanalysis
Is a psychology of surface.
Stay on the outside side.
My poor analyst
Suffered a stroke and became a needy child.
As to the inner life: let the maid.

How pathetic is a king who died of cancer
Rushing back after all these years to consult more doctors.
Escaped from the urn of his ashes in his pajamas.
Except in Islam you are buried in your body.
The Shah mounts the foal.
It is an honor.
He is in and out in a minute.
She later became my friend
And married a Texan.

I hurry to the gallery on the last day of the show
To a line stretching around the block in the rain—
For the Shah of sculptors, sculpture's virile king,
And his cold-rolled steel heartless tons.
The blunt magnificence stuns.
Cruelty has a huge following.
The cold-rolled steel mounts the foal.

The future of psychoanalysis is it has none.

I carry a swagger stick.
I eat a chocolate.
I eat brown blood.

When we drove with our driver on the highways of Ghana
To see for ourselves what the slave trade was,
Elmina was Auschwitz.
The slaves from the bush were marched to the coast
And warehoused in dungeons under St. George's Castle,
Then FedExed to their new jobs far away.

One hotel kept a racehorse as a pet.
The owner allowed it the run of the property.
Very shy, it walked standoffishly
Among the hotel guests on the walkways and under the palms.
The Shah had returned as a racehorse dropping mounds of caviar
Between a coconut grove and the Gulf of Guinea.

An English royal is taught to strut
With his hands clasped behind his back.
A racehorse in West Africa kept as a pet
Struts the same way the useless royals do,
Nodding occasionally to indicate he is listening.
His coat has been curried until he is glistening.

Would you rather be a horse without a halter
Than one winning races being whipped?
The finish line is at the starting gate, at St. George's Castle.
The starting gate is at the finish line for the eternal life.
God rears and whinnies and gives a little wave.
He would rather be an owner than a slave.

Someone fancy says
How marvelous money is.
Here I am, an admirer of Mahatma Gandhi,
Ready to praise making pots of money
And own a slave.
I am looking in the mirror as I shave the slave.
I shave the Shah.
I walk into the evening and start being charming.

A counterfeiter prints me.
(The counterfeiter *is* me.)
He prints Mohammad Reza Shah Pahlavi.

I call him Nancy.
He is so fancy.
It is alarming
He is so charming.
It is the thing he does and knows.
It is the fragrance of a rose.
It is the nostrils of his nose.
It is the poetry and prose.
It is the poetry.
It is a horse cab ride through Central Park when it snows.
It is Jackie Kennedy's hairpiece that came loose,
That a large Secret Service agent helped reattach.

I remember the Duck and Duckess of Windsor.
You could entertain them in your house.

Here I am, looking around the room
At everyone getting old except the young,
Discovering that I am lacking in vanity,
Not that I care, being debonair,
Delighted by an impairment of feeling
That keeps everything away,
People standing around in a display case
Even when they are in bed with you,
And laser-guided bombs destroy the buildings
Inside the TV, not that I care,
Not that I do not like it all,
Not that I am short or tall,
Not that I do not like to be alive,
And I appeal to you for pity,
Having in mind that you will read this
Under circumstances I cannot imagine
A thousand years from now.

Have pity on a girl, perdurable, playful,
And delicate as a foal, dutiful, available,

Who is waiting on a bed in a room in the afternoon for God.
His Majesty is on his way, who long ago has died.
She is a victim in the kingdom, and is proud.
Have pity on me a thousand years from now when we meet.
Open the mummy case of this text respectfully.
You find no one inside.

from *Raritan*

Country Western Singer

◇　　◇　　◇

I used to feel like a new man
After the day's first brew.
But then the new man I became
Would need a tall one too.

As would the new man he became,
And the new one after him.
And so on and so forth till the new men made
The dizzy room go dim.

And each one said, I'll be your muse,
I'll trade you song for beer:
He said, I'll be your salt lick, honey,
If you will be my deer.

He said, I'll be your happy hour,
And you, boy, you'll be mine
And mine won't end at six or seven
Or even at closing time.

Yes, son, I'll be your spirit guide;
I'll lead you to Absolut,
To Dewar's, Bushmills, and Jameson,
Then down to Old Tangle Foot.

And there I'll drain the pretense from you
That propped you up so high;
I'll teach you salvation's just
Salivation without the I.

To hear his sweet talk was to think
You'd gone from rags to riches,
Till going from drink to drink became
Like going from hags to bitches,

Like going from bed to barroom stool,
From stool to bathroom stall,
From stall to sink, from sink to stool,
From stool to hospital.

Now the monitors beep like pinball machines
And coldly the IV drips;
And a nurse runs a moistened washcloth over
My parched and bleeding lips,

And the blood I taste, the blood I swallow,
Is as far away from wine
As 5:10 is for the one who dies
At 5:09.

from *Virginia Quarterly Review*

Drawing Jesus

◇ ◇ ◇

The first patient drew Jesus as a tall, slender man with three smiling heads, one eye in the center of each. Another sketched him as a stick figure wearing a yellow hat. The teenage girl from Alabama drew a white vulture with a halo above its head. At the table by the window the Hungarian immigrant whose language no one understood drew a face with a scar running down his cheek, a ragged red beard, and the kind of wild eyes that frighten children. The old woman who has lived half-a-century in the asylum painted a picture of a dozen orange boxes and asked me to guess which one Jesus was hiding in. I pointed to the box with the bulge in the middle. The Hungarian started laughing. Then they all joined in.

from *Gulf Coast*

Money

◇   ◇   ◇

Coin Exhibit, British Museum.

Their misshapenness strikes the table in tiny splashes,
like still-cooling splatters of silver. Stater and shekel,
mina and obol. Persia's bullion had a lion and bull.

Athens an owl, Messana a hare, a jar for Terone, Melos
a pomegranate. Call it museum money, written off
and not expected back—some Ozymandian loose change,

or a bit of dodo boodle, bygone swag, has-been loot,
history's tithe to itself. And God knows after all this
gazing at glass maybe even you mull the quaintness

of things kept too long. But not so fast. This old currency
returns us to first principles, to a time when poverty
had heft, when debt was assigned its correct weight,

spilled metal coldcocking its solid clink against metal,
when taxes, rents and sundry dues were made real
by the real coins that paid for them, knurled and oblong,

dented and pinched, coins that called out your cost
when spoken on scales and so relentlessly palpable
they held their ground as outlaw selves of your reflective tact,

giving the middle finger to poetic truth. They belong
to days before dollars dipped, when it was futile to speculate
on the facts; ingots were unillusionary, would mean

what you spent, and prosperity, like perdition, properly
shouldered its burden, like those last Roman senators
forced to carry their assets in carts. Know what truth was?

Truth was the unapproximating mix of gold and silver
smelted and cast into bars, the alloy hammered flat,
blanks cut with shears, stacked, then hammered again

into circular shape. Now that's genuine, that's proof.
The heat and hiss, the loud crack of tools. When what you earned
was itself evidence of a life lived in labor, the stubble-

to-beard truth of busting your butt—a few, of course,
added bronze to phony the weight, but being neither metaphor
nor symbol, its quality could be checked by a chisel cut.

from *New American Writing*

What Every Soldier Should Know

◇   ◇   ◇

To yield to force is an act of necessity, not of will;
it is at best an act of prudence.
—Jean-Jacques Rousseau

If you hear gunfire on a Thursday afternoon,
it could be for a wedding, or it could be for you.

Always enter a home with your right foot;
the left is for cemeteries and unclean places.

O-guf! Tera armeek is rarely useful.
It means *Stop! Or I'll shoot.*

Sabah el khair is effective.
It means *Good Morning.*

Inshallah means *Allah be willing.*
Listen well when it is spoken.

You will hear the RPG coming for you.
Not so the roadside bomb.

There are bombs under the overpasses,
in trashpiles, in bricks, in cars.

There are shopping carts with clothes soaked
in foogas, a sticky gel of homemade napalm.

Parachute bombs and artillery shells
sewn into the carcasses of dead farm animals.

A graffiti sprayed onto the overpasses:
I will kell you, American.

Men wearing vests rigged with explosives
walk up, raise their arms and say *Inshallah.*

There are men who earn eighty dollars
to attack you, five thousand to kill.

Small children who will play with you,
old men with their talk, women who offer chai—

and any one of them
may dance over your body tomorrow.

from *American Poet*

ARTHUR VOGELSANG

The Family

◇   ◇   ◇

There is a trip over horizontal white and vertical blue lightning
Which can go low but can't go high to
Where Judy is sleeping confidently
And the pilot is sweating black water, his forehead some black steam.
Those around him say it is not actually black
But is like black or like you saw black.
They are sailing easily like sailing if you understand
There are no essential propelling moving parts
Only air passing over and turning the blades or sails or fans
In four tubes and they call these jets.
It is simple and safe and they are going fast
As you all have smoothly and the co-pilot is sweating, on his forehead,
Brown mud (very light brown, very thin, mud).
The attendant says it is not mud but reminds her of mud.

Why is the girl, who I know best, sleeping well?
Because they are sailing smoothly. Why are the pilots'
Bodies cooling them with disquieting jarring sweat?
Because they are passing over horizontal white and vertical blue lightning.

I'm tracking (on a good computer) this. Continental shows it
As a cartoon real plane over Indianapolis with dark gray jagged lines around it.
Later it will be over Harrisburg with light gray lines hopping around it.
Our dead daughter and our dead son
Are napping in the next room, through two archways.
How may that be? Why are the pilots
Emitting brown and black steam?
Are they reminded of their wars (each in different wars)

When the man-made light with bad intentions continued upw
        sometimes slightly faster
And sometimes slightly slower than they could go,
And boy could they go then, faster than the noise
Of words in a room person to person (you think it's simultaneous,
The sound of talking, don't you, until you think about it)
And sometimes the noise of no noise at all in the plane or in the room
Like two people sleeping in another room
Without moving for hours or you sleeping in a plane and then you w
        arrived
And they were here, awake and speaking to me,
Me the living, as if the living were on earth.

from *Colorado Review*

Coulrophobia

◇　　◇　　◇

Neither clown was especially trustworthy—their pranks ranged from exploding pens to, in an ugly custody case, propped-up buckets of battery acid—but they were good company and frankly I needed the laughs. I had just driven away another patient but not overly patient woman, and I was between jobs in the way that Catholics are between Messiahs. I had been trained in stock speculation, I was hoping to practice stock speculation again at some point, but I was preparing myself for a wait. So I started spending evenings—sometimes days and evenings—at the Vroom Room. The Vroom Room is a basement place in a part of Baltimore that I now associate almost entirely with abandoned tricycles, vomit, and licorice. At that point the bar was something of a clown training ground—a place for the harder-drinking clowns to pad around in their size 24 shoes and reflect on their acts, aperitifs in easy reach. By 2 a.m. they'd be hunched over the toilets—and, as none of the stalls had doors, the effect would be an EKG line of bobbing and vomiting clowns. I don't remember which clown I met first—Kicko, with his green snake wig and his "Rape Isn't Funny Unless You're Raping a Clown" T-shirt, or Laurence, whose raised eyebrows suggested a surprised stenographer. I don't remember how many times Laurence deadpanned the "Fuck you, clown!" joke, or how often Kicko recounted "The Aristocrats," with each new perversion more outlandish than the last. I remember the FBI raid, and the fun that the local newspapers and TV anchors had with the story. I remember how alone I felt afterward. I remember how, even months later, the Vroom Room's dishwashers couldn't rinse the liqueur glasses free of grease paint. But this is me at my most impatient—always blowing the punch line, the relationship— speculating recklessly, hurrying ahead—the living embodiment of Kicko's favorite joke, which went (and God bless Kicko):

"I'm the world's greatest comedian, ask me the secret of my success."
"OK, what's the secret of—"
"Timing."

from *Tarpaulin Sky*

Flu Song in Spanish

◊   ◊   ◊

God of the bees, god of gold keys, god of all in-
famous noses, I folded our total
in two today—I drove alone
and I walked away (as if each mile up your hill
were a letter in a word I'm inventing).
So I stuck my head in a hole and stood.
So far so. So far
good. Now I wear that hole like a hood
in a house
of inscrutable signals.

God of the guess, god of the gap
mind if I make you a martyr?
If the sky says anything, it's everything! at once!
(Nor did you answer my question.)
So I stick my head in a hole and stand. So far
so far. So far, grand. Sand in my pants and ants
in the box, I wish there were bells
for when I should stop. Show me the bell for when I should stop!
(Not that I'd know
when to ring it.)

Grant me the grace and I'll fix it. Shit.
My Father (that bitch!) he hides
at the head
of his third wife's table.
The man says one thing, then it's nothing
for months (though I've always been
welcome to dinner).

So I stook my head in a hole instead.
So far: slow car: sofa bed. A brick in the back
where he buries the dead. His task is her
two daughters.

God of the aster, God of disaster, God of
charisma and risk: if the word and the wing
are the same stringy thing
then what in the world will I say?
The sign means so much: you translate
my hunch (there's no chance
in hell today). So I stick my head in a hole and drown. So far
lost, so far
found: a bone-cutter's house in a blood-lit town—I swear
I'll tear your eyes away.

from *Alaska Quarterly Review*

Big

◇　◇　◇

I know when I buy it that it's big. And when the guy
who wheels it out, not on a dolly, but a flat-bed as long
as my truck—when that guy, with his Fu Manchu

and lifter's belt, won't try to move it, even with my help,
I know it's *really* big. And when the guy *he* calls
clumps up, and as he cinches on *his* belt, I shove,

and the thing won't budge, I know it's *too* big. Not
until, though, we hoist one edge onto my tailgate,
and for an instant, half its weight presses my knee

so hard I feel a bruise rising, straight-edged as the box—
not until then do I grasp half how big it is.
My fantasy—family and friends watching theater-style

movies in my den, popcorn and cappuccino courtesy
of me—collapses like my dream of surfing Malibu.
Somehow I thrashed to where the surfers bobbed,

relaxed as gulls on the broad-shouldered swells.
But my wave didn't break into a two-foot roil of chop
the way Galveston waves do, as if the sea has unrolled

a frothy white rug. It kept rising—a titanic
shoulder-shrug—and I knew it was too much wave:
too much mass, too much speed, too much water.

It was too much wrestler for me, too much marlin,
too large an army with too many missiles raining down.
It was too much fastball, too much free-fall,

too many tacklers, too few blockers, too many rules
of etiquette, far too many lawyers slithering into town.
It was too much thermodynamics and wind-chill,

too much calculus, too much interest on a mega-jumbo loan.
It was despair, genital shrinkage, intestinal out-rush,
earthquake on top of earthquake grinding me. Oh,

it was fear, fear, fear. I know, as that big TV crushes down,
I'll never make it do my bidding, or give me back
what used to be my home.

from *Michigan Quarterly Review*

The Home of the Brave

◇　◇　◇

—after the Nick Berg decapitation video

The home of the brave is a small room.
At first, it mimics us.
Armed men stand side by side.
They are aware of their power.
They have concealed their identities.
Only their leader speaks,
and he speaks at length,
reading from a prepared statement,
foregrounding their intentions
with weak rhetoric,
belief in God.
His comrades fidget and remain silent.
When the screaming begins,
the camera shakes
with a new honesty—
mimicry is done with now—
the men bear down,
and the home of the brave
is what we cannot understand,
what we cannot endure,
so long as we are free.

from *Sacramento News & Review*

From "Opposites" and "More Opposites"

◇ ◇ ◇

3

What is the opposite of *baby*?
The answer is *a grown-up,* maybe.

11

The opposite of *kite,* I'd say,
Is *yo-yo.* On a breezy day
You take your *kite* and let it *rise*
Upon its string into the skies,
And then you pull it *down* with ease
(Unless it crashes in the trees).
A *yo-yo,* though, drops *down,* and then
You quickly bring it *up* again
By pulling deftly on its string
(If you can work the blasted thing).

21

The opposites of *earth* are two,
And which to choose is up to you.
One opposite is called *the sky,*
And that's where larks and swallows fly;

But angels, there, are few if any,
Whereas in *heaven* there are many.
Well, which word are you voting for?
Do birds or angels please you more?
It's very plain that you are loath
To choose. All right, we'll keep them both.

from *American Poet*

At Dusk, the Catbird

◊   ◊   ◊

Twitched in the forsythia,
Hooked my eye and held it
Like a hackled lure cast out
From eroding sills of light.

Too bright
For that late hour, the bush
Ignited flower by flower to
Furnace-roar and glare where the bird

Alit, delicate.
Slender beak, sleek
Head cocked, tricked out in black
Array, he mimed the butler's clock-

Work of deft bows and plucked
One ladybug (*fly away home*)
From an amber cluster
Suppering on dew, then flew

Into the moon,
A throne away from home,
The bug his jeweled crown,
My eye his perilune.

from *The Vocabula Review*

An Experiment

◊   ◊   ◊

Lavoisier instructed his assistant
to conduct an experiment regarding the durability
of the brain's chemistry.

Lavoisier, the great chemist, had been
condemned to the guillotine, and he desired
nothing more than to know what was to become of him.

The assistant was instructed by Lavoisier
to count the number of attempted blinks of the disembodied eyes.
This number could be said to arrive

at the end of knowing.
This number would prove beyond doubt
the location of a mind.

The assistant did as he was told.
He came to the site.
He carried his notebook and pencil.

But the crowd was large and excited.
Vendors offered hot fried food, wine, and syrupy things
for children to drink.

The body was removed from its head.
The agent turned to the crowd,
the dripping head raised above his own.

The end of the beginning
of capital punishment by guillotine in France.
Lavoisier blinked—unfortunately the record

of the assistant was, due to the distraction
of the moment, somewhat imprecise—
between 13 and 15 times.

from *Crazyhorse*

Remiss Rebut

◇ ◇ ◇

Remiss rebut.
It is over and done for,
and the glory gone,
the seaweed foul,
the sea itself
a symbol in your dream.

Let it be,
and behind it all,
you will see
the globe,
an earth becoming slowly
a real world,
undreamed of but beheld.

from *Colorado Review*

CONTRIBUTORS' NOTES AND COMMENTS

KAZIM ALI was born in Croyden, England, in 1971. He is the author of a book of poetry, *The Far Mosque* (Alice James Books), and a novel, *Quinn's Passage* (BlazeVOX [books]). A founding editor of Nightboat Books, he teaches at Oberlin College and Stonecoast, the low-residency MFA program of the University of Southern Maine. His second book of poems, *The Fortieth Day,* is forthcoming in 2008 from BOA Editions.

Of "The Art of Breathing," Ali writes: "Classical vedantic thought, at the heart of my yoga practice, is full of the kind of paradoxes poems dream about. According to Swami Chinmayanda, within the innermost sheath of human existence where one would expect perhaps to find one's 'divine nature,' instead lie *vasanas*—the 'urges,' all the small ego trips and desires that separate the individual from Divine. In conflicting dharma stories told by Sri Krishnamacharya, a hero who recovers a stolen idol and the thief who took it are each regarded to be an avatar of Vishnu. The instigating premise of the Bhagavad Gita is an internecine war.

"I always wanted separate things to meet. Wasn't 'union'—the actual meaning of the word 'yoga'—the point of spiritual practice? Last July I was at a beach in Florida with my cousin Sakina. Sakina's mother had just passed away and we were talking about God and I wanted Sakina to see how at the horizon sometimes the ocean and the sky are indistinguishable, that all substance is the same; Lisel Mueller has described it as the way 'heaven pulls earth into its arms.' But that day at the beach the water was a luminous emerald green, streaked with rashes of purple from the midafternoon sky. The line between them at the horizon was stark and clear.

"This poem was written at the same time I was writing an essay called 'Yoga and the Cessation of the Self' on yoga and the poetry and suicide of Reetika Vazirani. My poem takes its title from an essay Vazirani published—ostensibly about yoga but actually, it seems, about her father's suicide. Yoga and poetry both confront a 'cessation of the self.' Often we are supposed to release ourselves—to language, to subject, to 'muse' or God. At the beginning of the Baghavad Gita, Arjuna refuses to fight his cousins, and so Krishna discourses on yoga and the Self. When we work to end our urges and desires, what is it that happens? And to whom?"

JEANNETTE ALLÉE was born in 1961 and grew up in Colorado and Idaho. She was a Foundation Scholar at the Evergreen State College, where she studied film and creative writing. She has received an Artist Trust grant, a 4Culture grant, and won a Richard Hugo House New Works competition. She has performed social critique monologues in Northwest venues including On the Boards. She is curator of Words' Worth, the poetry program of the Seattle City Council, and has recently completed a manuscript entitled "Eunuchs on their Lunch Hour."

Of "Crimble of Staines," Allée writes: "The title comes from the name of a car dealership in Surrey, UK (Staines is the town, Crimble the owner). When I was in England, I was struck by the snickersnack whiplash slap (or sigh) of the psychological landscape of their place names, businesses, language. With Crimble I had an almost plaintive sense of falling-apartedness. One afternoon, I met with a lawyer friend at the Groucho Club in London. Squiffily, he held forth on bachelor-hood, talking about the 'crumbling masonry' of his 'anti-relationship structure.' What writer could pass up that line? (He also said, 'I'm not depressed that you've been here three days and not slept with me, but that you haven't slept with *anybody*.')

"I used to rue my small-town upbringing (we learned to shoot rifles as a component of earth science), but the limitations only made me thirsty to know more, to go out and get life by the scruff of the neck."

RAE ARMANTROUT was born in Vallejo, California, in 1947. Her most recent book, *Next Life,* was published by Wesleyan in 2007. Her previous books include *Up to Speed* (Wesleyan, 2004), *Veil: New and Selected Poems* (Wesleyan, 2001), and *The Pretext* (Green Integer, 2001). Armantrout's poems have been included in *The Oxford Book of American Poetry* (Oxford, 2006), and in four previous editions of *The Best American Poetry.* She is a professor in the literature department at the University of California, San Diego.

Armantrout writes: "Part of the pleasure of poetry has always been the rather strange pleasure of 'calling one thing by another's name.' That's what metaphor does, after all. 'Scumble' asks about the psychology of this phenomenon. What is the kick in substitution? Is it covertly erotic?"

MARY JO BANG was born in Waynesville, Missouri, in 1946, and grew up in St. Louis. She is the author of four books of poetry, *Apology for Want* (University Press of New England, 1997), which won the Bakeless Prize; *Louise in Love* (Grove, 2001); *The Downstream Extremity of the Isle of Swans* (University of Georgia Press, 2001); and *The Eye Like a Strange Balloon* (Grove, 2004). Her fifth book of poems, *Elegy*, is forthcoming from Graywolf Press in October 2007. A graduate of the Columbia University MFA program, she is an associate professor of English and director of the creative writing program at Washington University in St. Louis.

Of "The Opening," Bang writes: "I wanted to write a sequence poem where the sequence wasn't so much an indication of duration, or forward motion where each new action is dependent on a prior one, but instead where sequence was an indicator of repetition. I wanted to suggest a small door one might open and look in to glimpse a shallow stage where a play continued ad infinitum. An adjacent prop room would hold an inexhaustible supply of objects and costumes. Each object untarnished, each costume unchanged from the day it was made. All the while, behind the viewer's back, is the world, that other stage, where things fall apart."

NICKY BEER, born in 1976, is from the Long Island town of Northport, New York. She received her BA from Yale University, her MFA from the University of Houston, and a PhD from the University of Missouri-Columbia. She received a 2007 literature fellowship from the National Endowment for the Arts and a 2006 Discovery/*The Nation* award. She is married to the poet Brian Barker. She lives in Columbia, Missouri.

Beer writes: "The poem 'Still Life with Half-Turned Woman and Questions' has two sources: W. S. Merwin's 'Some Last Questions' from *The Lice*, which Bruce Beasley refers to as an 'anti-catechism,' and 'Interior with Sitting Woman' (1910) by Danish painter Vilhelm Hammershoi, whose best-known work consists of sparse domestic interiors, often featuring a solitary woman with her back turned to the viewer. For me, there was something in the visual reticence of the painting that was reminiscent of the aloof, sinister speaker of Merwin's poem; adopting the form and something of the tone of the original poem allowed the painting's 'answers' to surface, but without diminishing the enigmatic quality of the art itself."

MARVIN BELL was born in New York City in 1937 and grew up in Center Moriches, on the south shore of eastern Long Island. Now retired from the Iowa Writers' Workshop, he serves on the faculty of the low-residency MFA program based at Pacific University in Oregon. His nineteenth book, *Mars Being Red,* will appear this year from Copper Canyon Press. He has created the form known as the "dead man poem," for which he is both famous and infamous. Previous collections of poetry include seven books from Atheneum and six from Copper Canyon, including *Iris of Creation* (1990), *The Book of the Dead Man* (1994), *Nightworks* (2000), and *Rampant* (2004). He and his wife, Dorothy, live in Iowa City, Iowa, and Port Townsend, Washington.

Bell writes: " 'The Method' is one of a number of wartime poems in the collection *Mars Being Red.* Its occasion is a beheading. The beheadings of prisoners has struck deep into the American psyche with its dread of anticipation, the instantaneousness of the act, the careless afterward, and the tension between needing to know and hardly daring to. Given the increasingly climactic nature of the headlines, one might come to feel that the tautological sublimity so prized by the *artiste* must wait. I have long wished to delineate the moment when the most explicit daily news merges with the epiphanic life of the mind, the impingements of the sensate with an overarching consciousness. The issue embedded in rough news is what to make of it—in both senses of that phrase. 'The Method' is a brief but intense example."

CHRISTIAN BÖK was born in Etobicoke, Ontario, in 1966. He is the author of *Eunoia* (Coach House Books, 2001), which won the Griffin Prize for Poetic Excellence (2002). *Crystallography* (Coach House Press, 1994), his first book of poetry, also earned a nomination for the Gerald Lampert Memorial Award (1995). He has created artificial languages for two television shows: Gene Roddenberry's *Earth: Final Conflict* and Peter Benchley's *Amazon.* Bök has also earned accolades for his performances of sound poetry. His conceptual artworks (which include books built out of Rubik's Cubes and LEGO bricks) have appeared at the Marianne Boesky Gallery in New York City as part of the exhibit "Poetry Plastique." He teaches in the department of English at the University of Calgary.

Bök writes: " 'Vowels' is an anagrammatic text, permuting the fixed array of letters found only in the title. 'Vowels' appears in my book *Eunoia,* a lipogrammatic suite of stories, in which each vowel appears by itself in its own chapter."

LOUIS E. BOURGEOIS was born in 1970 in New Orleans, Louisiana, and raised in the Slidell-LaCombe area, as well as East New Orleans on

Bayou Sauvage. In 1996 he earned a BA from Louisiana State University in English and in 2002 was the first graduate of the University of Mississippi's MFA program in creative writing. In 2004 he was the winner of the University of Milwaukee's *Cream City Review*'s poetry contest for his poem "The Shed: The Daughter of Shadows Speaks from Max Beckmann's *The Dream* (1921)." His books include *Through the Cemetery Gates, The Distance of Ducks, The Animal, Cora Falling Off the Face of the Earth, White Night, Fragments of a Life Thirty-two Years Gone, OLGA,* and a forthcoming collection of short prose, *The Gar Diaries.* He is cofounder and editor of *VOX,* an independent experimental literary journal based in Oxford, Mississippi.

Bourgeois writes: " 'A Voice from the City' is my first attempt at writing a surrealist poem in the context of an historical event. It is an introduction to an internal dialogue from the perspective of a middle-class Cambodian child who is caught in Phnom Penh during the invasion of the Khmer Rouge in April of 1975.

"Hence, 'A Voice from the City' is a mere fragment of a much longer prose poem sequence that I hope to complete in the coming year."

GEOFFREY BROCK was born in Atlanta, Georgia, in 1964. He is the author of *Weighing Light: Poems* (Ivan R. Dee, 2005), the translator of Cesare Pavese's *Disaffections: Complete Poems 1930–1950* (Copper Canyon, 2002), and the editor of the forthcoming *Anthology of Twentieth-Century Italian Poetry* (Farrar, Straus and Giroux, 2008). He has received fellowships from the National Endowment for the Arts, the Academy of American Poets, and the Guggenheim Foundation, and he was recently a Wallace Stegner Fellow at Stanford. He now teaches creative writing and translation at the University of Arkansas in Fayetteville, where he lives with his wife, the writer Padma Viswanathan, and their son, Ravi. His website is www.geoffreybrock.com.

Brock writes: " 'Flesh of John Brown's Flesh' was written a few years ago during a residency at the Virginia Center for the Creative Arts. As VCCA is not far from Harpers Ferry, and I was working on a series (still in progress) of 'historical poems,' Brown was much on my mind. I was researching haphazardly, looking for an angle of approach, when I came across an account by his eldest son, John Brown, Jr., of Brown's household code of punishment. That account, from which many of the poem's details are lifted, paints a portrait of paternal authority and sacrifice that is both severe and weirdly tender. It offered me a way of seeing and framing Brown's final sacrificial act, which still has much to teach us about the difficulty of defining terrorism and madness in places where the status quo is terrifying and mad."

MATTHEW BYRNE was born in Chicago, Illinois, in 1973. He is a broker at a Chicago insurance agency. He has a BA in English from the University of Iowa, and an MFA in poetry from the University of Montana.

Byrne writes: " 'Let Me Count the Ways' is an expression of my preoccupation with how self-interest infiltrates the realm of affection. While writing the poem I began to think that perhaps affection and self-interest are less at odds than they are symbiotic, and to embrace—or, at very least, to accept—this notion is to see with more clarity the nature of how we identify with what we cherish. So what started as a rather dark conceit wound up, for me, a playful exercise in examining my nostalgia for the mountains I moved away from when I left Montana."

MACGREGOR CARD was born in Los Angeles in 1974. He graduated with a BA in literature from the University of California, Santa Cruz, and an MFA in poetry from Brown University. He edits *Firmilian: A Spasmodic Knowledge Base* (www.firmilian.blogspot.com) and with Andrew Maxwell is coeditor of *The Germ: A Journal of Poetic Research* (www.germspot.blogspot.com).

Card writes: " 'Duties of an English Foreign Secretary' is the title poem of a recently completed manuscript. It is also the title of an essay written in 1852 by the English poet Sydney Dobell, chief among the group of British poets who came to be derided as the Spasmodic School. Dobell was more radical than his Pre-Raphaelite successors. His convulsive turns of imagery and his near unpredicated use of gesture, exaggeration, and repetition (typical are lines such as 'Ah weary, weary day / Oh weary, weary day / Oh, day so weary, oh, day so dreary / Oh weary, weary, weary, weary / Oh, weary, weary!') made him a favorite object of derision in magazines such as *Blackwood's*. The success of his detractors was so absolute, in fact, that not one of Dobell's works has been reprinted since the Victorian era.

"The poem wanders from Dobell's essay, a spasmodic meditation on politics and philosophy. None of its language is taken from that text."

JULIE CARR was born in Cambridge, Massachusetts, in 1966. She danced professionally in New York City from 1988 to 2000 and holds a PhD in English from the University of California, Berkeley. She has published two books of poetry, *Mead: An Epithalamion* (University of Georgia

Press, 2004) and *Equivocal* (Alice James Books, 2007). She teaches English and creative writing at the University of Colorado at Boulder and is the copublisher, with Tim Roberts, of Counterpath Press. She lives with her husband and two children in Denver, Colorado.

Carr writes: "The poem 'marriage' has had so many permutations that its source is no longer any particular lived or imagined experience. Its sources are instead its previous selves. The phonic and semantic relationships among the words 'marriage,' 'edge,' 'manna,' and 'mannered' have been, throughout, constant points of interest."

MICHAEL COLLIER was born in Phoenix, Arizona, in 1953 and is the author of five books of poems, including most recently *Dark Wild Realm* (Houghton Mifflin, 2006). *The Ledge* (Houghton Mifflin, 2000) was a finalist for the National Book Critics Circle Award and the *Los Angeles Times* Book Prize. The recipient of Guggenheim, National Endowment for the Arts, and Thomas Watson fellowships, he teaches English at the University of Maryland and serves as the director of the Bread Loaf Writers' Conference, Middlebury College. He is a former Poet Laureate of Maryland.

Of "Common Flicker," Collier writes: "During the spring, for several years running, a common flicker has announced its return to the neighborhood I live in outside of Baltimore by drumming on the metal cap of a defunct woodstove pipe that sticks out from the roof of my study. The pipe is no longer connected to a stove, so it conducts the incomparably loud sound directly and startlingly into my study. Flickers and woodpeckers do not sing. Their beaks, normally used for foraging insects from bark and dying trees, are how they create their 'song.' I don't keep a journal with much regularity, but when the bird appeared for the third spring, I began keeping track of its arrival. It turned out to be extremely punctual, showing up almost a year to the day of its previous appearance. 'Common Flicker' not only wants to celebrate the return of this bird, but it tries to approximate something of the furious, percussive, and uncompromising register of its song."

BILLY COLLINS was born in the French Hospital in New York City in 1941. His books of poetry include *The Trouble with Poetry and Other Poems* (Random House, 2005), a collection of haiku titled *She Was Just Seventeen* (Modern Haiku Press, 2006), *Nine Horses* (Random House, 2002), *Sailing Alone Around the Room: New and Selected Poems* (Random House, 2001), *Picnic, Lightning* (University of Pittsburgh Press, 1998),

The Art of Drowning (University of Pittsburgh Press, 1995), and *Questions About Angels* (William Morrow, 1991), which was selected for the National Poetry Series by Edward Hirsch and reprinted by the University of Pittsburgh Press in 1999. He is the editor of *Poetry 180: A Turning Back to Poetry* (Random House, 2003). He is a Distinguished Professor of English at Lehman College (City University of New York). A frequent contributor and former guest editor of *The Best American Poetry* series, he served as United States Poet Laureate from 2001 to 2003.

Of "The News Today," Collins writes: "It's not nice to speak ill of the dead, but Catullus has been dead for so long—he was born over a century before the Crucifixion—and his poems are so nasty, that such respectful truisms can be suspended in his case. Feared in his own time by his fellow sybarites in the waning years of the Roman Republic, he was not fully translated into English until the fifteenth century; and since then, his poems, despite other distinguishing marks, notably his complex metrics, have been known chiefly for their jovial obscenities. Only a few of his upper-class contemporaries, such as his darling Lesbia, managed to escape the flinging of his ink-tipped darts. Caesar and Mamurra are a 'pair of shameless buggers'; Ameana's a 'fucked-out little scrubber'; and some poor fellow's date has 'the face of a French poodle'—an inspired anachronism in Peter Green's new translation. His short, stinging poems feature a 'consumptive tart,' a 'predictable bitch,' and a 'pissed-on whore.' In a rare mood of generosity, he pays a friend the strange compliment of having an asshole as clean as a polished saltshaker.

" 'The News Today' was prompted by the appearance last year of Green's lively bilingual edition. I must have thought it high time, especially in these days of polite poetry (not you, Bukowski), that the classical put-down artist got a taste of his own rude medicine."

ROBERT CREELEY was born in Arlington, Massachusetts, in 1926. He was educated at Harvard University (1943–46) and later at Black Mountain College, where he formed a close alliance with Charles Olson. Key books by Creeley were published by Scribner in the 1960s and 1970s: *For Love* (1962), *Words* (1967), *Pieces* (1969), *A Day Book* (1972), and the *Selected Poems* of 1976. Other collections include *So There: Poems 1976–1983* (1998) and *Just in Time: Poems 1984–1994* (2001), both from New Directions. *Tales Out of School,* a book of selected interviews, came out in the University of Michigan Press's Poets on Poetry series in 1993. Creeley edited Charles Olson's *Selected Writings* (New Directions, 1967) as well as volumes devoted to Walt Whitman (Penguin, 1973) and

Robert Burns (Ecco, 1989). He held a titled professorship at the State University of New York at Buffalo for twenty-five years beginning in 1978. He was the guest editor of *The Best American Poetry 2002*. In his introduction to that volume, he brought up the vexing question of "whether or not there is finally the 'best' of anything." He decided that the poems he had chosen were "*better* than the best, each and every one of them. If you don't agree, then go find your own—which is not offered as a challenge. Rather as fact of what, one has to recognize, is the point of any of this to begin with, that we are 'instructed, moved, and delighted' by poetry, as Pound said, quoting Agricola, who had said it centuries before him." Robert Creeley died on March 30, 2005.

In the Spring 2006 issue of *Beloit Poetry Journal*, Kate Cumiskey offers a remembrance of Creeley, who was her mentor at the Atlantic Center for the Arts in New Smyrna Beach, Florida. Shortly before his death, Creeley visited the University of North Carolina in Wilmington, where Cumiskey was a student. Creeley wrote "Dover Beach (Again)" and dedicated it "for Kate" on February 10, 2005:

> The waves keep at it.
> Arnold's Aegean Sophocles heard,
> the swell and ebb,
> the cresting and the falling under,
>
> each one particular and the same—
> Each day a reminder, each sun in its world, each face,
> each word something one hears
> or someone once heard.

LINH DINH was born in Saigon, Vietnam, in 1963, came to the United States in 1975, and has also lived in Italy and England. He is the author of two collections of stories, *Fake House* (Seven Stories Press, 2000) and *Blood and Soap* (Seven Stories Press, 2004), and four books of poems, *All Around What Empties Out* (Tinfish, 2003), *American Tatts* (Chax, 2005), *Borderless Bodies* (Factory School, 2006), and *Jam Alerts* (Chax, 2007). His work has been anthologized in the 2000 and 2004 editions of *The Best American Poetry* and in *Great American Prose Poems: From Poe to the Present*. Linh Dinh has edited the anthologies *Night, Again: Contemporary Fiction from Vietnam* (Seven Stories Press, 1996) and *Three Vietnamese Poets* (Tinfish, 2001). He has also translated, in *Night, Fish and Charlie Parker*, the poetry of Phan Nhien Hao (Tupelo Press, 2006). His poems and stories have been translated into Italian, Spanish, Portuguese, German, Japanese, and Arabic. He has also published widely in Vietnamese.

Of "Continuous Bullets over Flattened Earth" and "A Super-Clean Country," Dinh writes: "Crazy Jane said to the anal bishop, 'Fair and foul are near of kin / And fair needs foul.' Then, 'Love has pitched his mansion in / The place of excrement; / For nothing can be sole or whole / That has not been rent.' Whole we're certainly not, yet our renting is continuous. We can grant neither fair nor foul their right proportions, but must exaggerate both, with special effects, airbrush and pixels, into frightful perversions, yet nothing fazes us, we're cool. Having given the world the assembly line, we've converted ourselves into efficient, interchangeable chumps, into machines, in short. Stay cool, keep cool, be cool, act cool, even as one is suffering or inflicting pain. It's only shock and awe, y'all. In spite of the jiggling evidences at every foodcourt, our bodies are no longer flesh, flab or cellulite, but steel-tough and glistening, a square-cornered, gas-guzzling 24/7 boner, a monster truck in loose-fitting jeans, until we enter the smallest room, of course. Consider that más macho Hemingway wrote standing up, but often read sitting down, on a commode, next to which he had installed a bookcase. This practice of ingesting literature while digesting stuff is hardly universal, although de rigueur in the homeland, where one can scan a commody *New Yorker* poem or two while being tucked away in a roomette or stall of one's own, shielded from workplace bullshit or domestic mayhem. A wise, productive use of one's down time, uplifting and more cultured than a glory hole, it's also a way to repudiate the very act of commoding. Vallejo, 'Doubt your feces for a moment.' It's not a problem, César, since we never believed it in the first place. Reading while commoding doesn't just ruin the reading experience, it debases commoding."

MIKE DOCKINS was born in 1972 and grew up in Yonkers, New York. He holds a BS from SUNY Brockport (1999) and an MFA from the University of Massachusetts Amherst (2002). He lives in Atlanta, where he is completing a doctorate at Georgia State University. He is a founding editor of *Redactions: Poetry & Poetics*. His first collection of poems, *Slouching in the Path of a Comet,* was published by Sage Hill Press in 2007. He also appears with his band, Clop.

Dockins writes: " 'Dead Critics Society' is one of seven or eight double abecedarians (some of them 'backwards') that I wrote a few years ago, each a sort of zany dramatic monologue. I'd read a single abecedarian in *Nimrod*—one with erratic line lengths; it seemed to me that the poem was not trying hard enough. Competitive as I am, I thought, 'I can top this,' and the project was launched. The most challenging aspect of the form was making the line lengths relatively even, so that the poem resembles a prose paragraph. This poem in particular came about after feeling frustrated by the established idea that all poems are *necessarily* about death. And Browning's word 'zooks' (from his dramatic monologue 'Fra Lippo Lippi') was a perfect opening for the speaker's tirade. This poem could be the only one in which Robert Browning's skeleton lurks under someone's bed—I'll have to look that up. I have been called 'irreverent' (amen) and here I live up to that by having fun at the expense not only of the Romantic poets but also of my education, for which, believe it or not, I am thankful."

SHARON DOLIN was born in Brooklyn, New York, in 1956. She received her BA and PhD from Cornell University and an MA from the University of California, Berkeley. She is the author of three books of poems: *Realm of the Possible* (Four Way Books, 2004), *Serious Pink* (Marsh Hawk Press, 2003), and *Heart Work* (The Sheep Meadow Press, 1995), as well as five chapbooks. In 1995 she founded the Center for Book Arts Letterpress Poetry Chapbook Competition, which she continues to direct, along with a Broadsides Reading Series at The Center in New York City. Since 1996 she has taught poetry seminars and workshops at the Unterberg Poetry Center of the 92nd Street Y; she also teaches at Poets House. She is currently poet-in-residence at Eugene Lang College, the New School for Liberal Arts in New York City.

Of "Tea Lay," Sharon Dolin writes: "I have always been in love with homophonic verse, a kind of 'ear poetry.' That is, I listen to a primary text and let my ear lead me, in part, to writing a poem based on the sounds of another poem. One summer, suffering from writer's block, I read John Clare's sonnets, with their agrarian-based nineteenth-century vision and language, and decided to treat them as though they were written in a foreign tongue. I used the sound bites of the poems as ir/reverently as a musician sampling other music. 'Tea Lay' is one sonnet from the 'Clare-Hewn' sequence. Chance and the dictionary, as well as my associations to word-sounds, all played a part in what I hope are independent poems that teeter on the brink of sense."

DENISE DUHAMEL was born in Providence, Rhode Island, in 1961, and grew up in Woonsocket, Rhode Island. She was educated at Emerson College (BFA) and Sarah Lawrence College (MFA). Her most recent books are *Two and Two* (University of Pittsburgh Press, 2005), *Mille et un sentiments* (Firewheel Editions, 2005), and *Queen for a Day: Selected and New Poems* (University of Pittsburgh Press, 2001). She is coeditor, with Maureen Seaton and David Trinidad, of *Saints of Hysteria: A Half-Century of Collaborative American Poetry* (Soft Skull, 2007). An associate professor at Florida International University in Miami, she is married to the visual poet Nick Carbó.

Of "Language Police Report," Duhamel writes: "After a lively discussion about political correctness, authenticity, author responsibility, and censorship, my extremely talented MFA student John Camacho (who has since graduated) sent me a list of banned words, as well as stereotypes to be avoided, issued by major educational publishers. The list was first published in Diane Ravitch's essay 'Language Police,' in the March 2003 issue of *The Atlantic*. Reprinted in her book *The Language Police: How Pressure Groups Restrict What Students Learn,* these guidelines—used by writers, editors, and illustrators of kindergarten through high school textbooks—are both horrifying and hilarious. I gave myself an assignment to use as many of these words as I possibly could in a prose poem. There were so many words, though, that the prose poem splintered into two—the one reprinted here and another called 'Avoidance,' which concentrated on words deemed as degrading to *old* (banned as an adjective that implies helplessness, dependency, or other negative qualities) people. Some of the concepts I failed to include in either prose poem—lumberjack (banned as sexist; replace with 'woodcutter'); junk bonds, polo, and yacht (all banned as elitist); and West (banned as Eurocentric)—are still up for grabs. John Camacho is busy at work on that poem."

STEPHEN DUNN was born on June 24, 1939, in Forest Hills, New York. He is the Distinguished Professor of Creative Writing (semiretired) at Richard Stockton College of New Jersey. He has written fourteen books of poetry. *Everything Else in the World* (W. W. Norton) includes "Where He Found Himself." *Different Hours* won the 2001 Pulitzer Prize. Dunn was awarded an Academy Award in Literature from the American Academy of Arts and Letters in 1995. He lives in Frostburg, Maryland, with his wife, the writer Barbara Hurd.

Of "Where He Found Himself," Dunn writes: "A few years ago I came across an uncharacteristic poem by David Ignatow, an untitled prose poem, in his *Selected Poems*. In it, a man who thinks he's going to die is assured by a strange voice that he will have a different fate: he is being turned into a zebra. The man is a misanthrope, and this transformation is going to make him—for lack of a better term—more compassionate. That's a great simplification of it, but it's a wonderful seriocomic poem, full of surprising moves, and I had it in mind when I was writing 'Where He Found Himself,' an uncharacteristic poem for me. I hope my poem creates its own fabulous terms and has its peculiar resonances."

RUSSELL EDSON was born in Stamford, Connecticut, in 1935. His books include *The Tunnel: Selected Poems* (Oberlin College Press, 1994), *The Tormented Mirror* (University of Pittsburgh Press, 2001), and *The House of Sara Loo* (Rain Taxi, 2002). He is a leading practitioner of the prose poem. He has compared the form to "a cast-iron aeroplane that can actually fly, mainly because its pilot doesn't seem to care if it does or not." He lives in Connecticut with his wife, Frances.

Of "See Jack," Edson writes: "My work is so distant from the life I know and live; otherwise, why write? I draw from the impersonal, the every-man-of-us, part of the brain. How the brain processes experience is set aside for the experience of the poem. The writing of the poem is the experience. As such, it remains as mysterious or unknown to me as it might to any other reader. So-called self-expression bores me, that is, poems that are written with a purpose; that self-consciousness to make words do something. A poem should fall as naturally, and with as much ambition, as an idle thought. So there is really nothing to say about Jack, but just to see him."

ELAINE EQUI was born in Oak Park, Illinois, in 1953. Her books include *Voice-Over* (1998), which won a San Francisco State Poetry Center Award; *The Cloud of Knowable Things* (2003); and most recently, *Ripple Effect: New & Selected Poems* (2007), all from Coffee House Press. She lives in New York City, where she teaches at New York University and in the MFA programs at the New School and City College.

Of "Etudes," Equi writes: "I rarely write in rhyme and am especially proud of this poem since every line in it rhymes. I also think the way the lines in each quatrain repeat (last one becoming first with others following consecutively) emphasizes the mechanical, cyclical flow of one season into the next. So many works of art revolve around one or more of the seasons. I love Botticelli's *Primavera,* Keats's 'To Autumn,' Wallace Stevens's 'The Snow Man,' Vivaldi's violin concertos, Jasper Johns's and Cy Twombly's stunning paintings. You would think with so much already written, sung, and painted about them, the idea would become hackneyed, but I haven't found that to be the case. In fact, with the increased threat of global warming, maybe we're in for a whole new revisionist view of 'the seasons.' One can only hope it's not too radical a departure from the original."

LANDIS EVERSON was born in Coronado, California, in 1926. With such friends as Jack Spicer and Robin Blaser, he participated actively in the Berkeley Renaissance of the late 1940s and 1950s. Everson wrote poems as a young man—some of which appeared in such journals as *Poetry, Kenyon Review,* and *Locus Solus*—but suspended the practice for forty-three years, resuming with a flourish four years ago. *Everything Preserved: Poems 1955–2005,* edited by Ben Mazer, was published by Graywolf Press in 2006 as the winner of the Emily Dickinson first-book award from the Poetry Foundation (to honor a poet of distinction over the age of fifty who has yet to publish a book). Nine poems in the volume date from the 1950s; the other sixty-six are from 2003 and since. Everson lives in San Luis Obispo, California.

Ben Mazer, Everson's editor during these past three years, says of him: "One of the remarkable things about Landis's return to poetry is the avidness with which he has followed what is happening. His energy for seeking out and reading obscure literary periodicals exceeds that of many younger men. Landis came of age in the heyday of the chapbook and the underground literary magazine, and his curiosity reflects that. It was especially a delight to introduce him to the many poets in New York and Boston whom he had the opportunity to read with on his trips east. As with his old friend John Ashbery, Landis has remained in contact with many of these poets."

THOMAS FINK was born in New York City in 1954 and was educated at Princeton (BA) and Columbia (PhD). His four books of poetry are *Surprise Visit* (Domestic Press, 1993), *Gossip* (Marsh Hawk Press, 2001), *After Taxes* (Marsh Hawk Press, 2004), and *No Appointment Necessary* (Moria Poetry, 2006). He has also written an e-chapbook, *Staccato Landmark* (Beard of Bees Press, 2006), as well as two books of criticism, including *A Different Sense of Power: Problems of Community in Late-Twentieth-Century U.S. Poetry* (Fairleigh Dickinson University Press, 2001). He is coeditor of *Literature Around the Globe* (Kendall/Hunt, 1994) with Tuzyline Jita Allan and coeditor of *"Burning Interiors": David Shapiro's Poetry and Poetics* (Fairleigh Dickinson University Press, 2007) with Joseph Lease. Fink's paintings hang in various collections. He is professor of English at City University of New York–LaGuardia.

Of "Yinglish Strophes IX," Fink writes: "Pogroms caused my grandmother Ethel Landsman (1888–1986), born in Odessa, Russia, of Jewish parentage, to come to the United States in 1905. I embrace Nichiren Shoshu Buddhism, not her faith, but recognizing Ethel as bearer of my Jewish *cultural* inheritance, I jotted down her spoken or written phrases and sentences for a decade. Versions of 'The Ethel Landsman Poems' in my first two books collage her utterances while, I suppose, spotlighting her *persona*. However, the 'Yinglish Strophes' series—now fifteen poems, spanning my latest two books, an e-chapbook, and beyond—is intended to emphasize multiple significations resulting from a Yiddish impact on English syntax, to add my own discourse, and to incorporate suggestions of social contexts available only after her passing. (Leo J. Rosten coined the term 'Yinglish,' exemplifying this syntactical migration.) By entertaining varied perspectives on interpersonal and intergroup conflict and by disrupting continuity between successive sentences, 'Yinglish Strophes IX,' I hope, foregrounds heterogeneous linguistic elements rather than an individual 'voiceprint.' "

HELEN RANSOM FORMAN was born in 1922, the daughter of John Crowe Ransom. Written between 1943 and 1950, "Daily" and five other poems of hers appeared in the *Michigan Quarterly Review* last year. In the periodical, the poems were erroneously attributed to John Crowe Ransom, because they were found in his archives in the Heard Library at Vanderbilt University, and the undated typescripts had no name on them. The editor's note in the *Michigan Quarterly Review* begins by quoting the *Norton Anthology of Modern Poetry*: "John Crowe Ransom's poetry could never be taken for anybody else's." Helen Ransom Forman continues to make her home in Gambier, Ohio, where her father taught for many years and edited *The Kenyon Review.*

LOUISE GLÜCK was born in New York City in 1943. She is the author of eleven books of poetry including, most recently, *Averno* (Farrar, Straus, and Giroux, 2006). She has won the Pulitzer Prize, the Bollingen Prize, and the National Book Critics Circle Award. She has also published a collection of essays, *Proofs and Theories: Essays on Poetry* (Ecco Press, 1994). For many years she taught at Williams College. She now teaches at Yale University and lives in Cambridge, Massachusetts. She was guest editor of *The Best American Poetry 1993.*

Of "Archaic Fragment," Glück writes: "I wrote the poem as a comic reprimand to myself after reading a group of Dana Levin's poems that talk about the problem of embodiment—being citizen of a body, and how hard that is—with such a passion for the physical world. I felt, in the presence of those poems, the envy that you feel in the presence of something important, and wished to emulate, as far as I could, her accomplishment."

ALBERT GOLDBARTH was born in Chicago, Illinois, in 1948, and lives in Wichita ("the Gateway to Boredom") Kansas. He is Distinguished Professor of Humanities in the Department of English at Wichita State University. He has published a novel and five collections of essays, the most recent of which, *Griffin,* appeared this year from Essay Press. He has been publishing volumes of poetry (from trade publishers, university publishers, and independent literary presses) for thirty-five years; two of these have received the National Book Critics Circle Award. His most recent book of poems is *The Kitchen Sink: New and Selected Poems 1972–2007,* from Graywolf Press. A self-described "complete computer refusenik," Goldbarth writes that his "fingertips have never touched a computer keyboard."

Goldbarth writes: "Really, it isn't laziness or aloofness or knee-jerk curmudgeonliness that keeps me from commenting on the poem, but a deep and clear desire for the work to stand on its own. You know—as for Keats and Dickinson and other actual heroic figures, from before the *American Idol*-ization of poetry."

DONALD HALL was born in New Haven, Connecticut, in 1928. He lives on a farm in New Hampshire and supports himself by freelance writing. His fourteenth book of poems, *The Painted Bed,* appeared from Houghton Mifflin in 2002, and in 2006 the same publisher issued *White Apples and the Taste of Stone: Selected Poems 1946–2006.* Besides poetry, Hall has written books on baseball, the sculptor Henry Moore, and the poet Marianne Moore; children's books, including *Ox-Cart Man* (1979), which won the Caldecott Medal; short stories; and plays. He has edited more than two dozen textbooks and anthologies, including *The Oxford Book of Children's Verse in America* (1990), *The Oxford Book of American Literary Anecdotes* (1981), *New Poets of England and America* (with Robert Pack and Louis Simpson, 1957), and *Contemporary American Poetry* (1962; revised 1972). He served as poetry editor of *The Paris Review* from 1953 to 1962. In June 2006 he was named Poet Laureate of the United States. He was the guest editor of *The Best American Poetry 1989.*

Of "The Master," Hall writes: "Over the years, I have not written many poems about poetry, but there is one called 'The Poem' and another called 'This Poem.' In 'The Master' I took some of Meister Eckhardt's sentences, mainly about God, and used them as a way of thinking about poetry. I am struck by the apparent distance between a poem and a poet's conscious being."

MARK HALLIDAY was born in Ann Arbor, Michigan, in 1949. He believes that he is not just a lightweight satirist. His books of poems are *Little Star* (William Morrow, 1987), *Tasker Street* (University of Massachusetts Press, 1992, winner of the Juniper Prize), *Selfwolf* (University of Chicago Press, 1999), and *Jab* (University of Chicago Press, 2002). His critical study *Stevens and the Interpersonal* was published by Princeton University Press in 1991. He has won a Lila Wallace–Reader's Digest Writers' Award, the Rome Prize of the American Academy of Arts and Letters, and a Guggenheim Fellowship. He teaches at Ohio University.

Of "Best Am Po," Halliday writes: "If I'd known that this poem would end up in *The Best American Poetry,* I would have made it even more ambitious."

FORREST HAMER was born in Goldsboro, North Carolina, in 1956. A psychologist living in Oakland, California, he is an affiliate member of the San Francisco Psychoanalytic Institute and Society. He was educated at Yale and Berkeley. His books of poems are *Call and Response* (Alice James, 1995), *Middle Ear* (Roundhouse Press, 2000), and *Rift* (Four Way Books, 2007). This is his third appearance in *The Best American Poetry.*

Hamer writes: " 'Initiation' alludes to several failures of speaking—in a self's speaking of and to itself; a mother's concern about her son's inexplicable anger; a future writer's frustration with the limits of his language; some boys' communication of powerlessness and welcome. I often wonder if violence, especially extraordinary violence, represents the ultimate failure of speaking 'the right words in the right order.' Moreover, I question if our very human struggles with aggression aren't finally integral to our capacity to create."

MATTHEA HARVEY was born in Bad Homburg, Germany, in 1973. She teaches poetry at Sarah Lawrence College and is a contributing editor for *jubilat* and *BOMB.* She is the author of *Modern Life* (Graywolf Press, 2007), *Sad Little Breathing Machine* (Graywolf Press, 2004), and *Pity the Bathtub Its Forced Embrace of the Human Form* (Alice James Books, 2001). Her first children's book, *The Little General and the Giant Snowflake,* illustrated by Elizabeth Zechel, is forthcoming from Soft Skull Press. She lives in Brooklyn, New York.

Harvey writes: " 'The Future of Terror/Terror of the Future 7' is an excerpt from a two-part series in my most recent book of poems, *Modern Life*. The poems were inspired by a desire to clarify what vague phrases like 'the future of terror' actually mean. To begin them, I made lists of the words that appear in the dictionary between 'future' and 'terror.' The 'Future of Terror' sections move from 'future' to 'terror,' while the 'Terror of the Future' sections move in reverse, from 'terror' to 'future.' I consider the series a modified abecedarius, and I've written an essay about the experience of writing in that form (along with a discussion of other abecedarian work by Edward Gorey, Tom Gauld, Blackalicious, Carolyn Forché, and Harryette Mullen), which can be found on my website at http://www.mattheaharvey.info."

ROBERT HASS was born in San Francisco in 1941. His most recent book is *Now & Then: The Poet's Choice Columns, 1997–2000* (Shoemaker & Hoard). A new book of his poems, *Time and Materials,* is forthcoming from Ecco/HarperCollins. He teaches at the University of California, Berkeley. He was the guest editor of *The Best American Poetry 2001.*

Of "Bush's War," Hass writes: "I was completely taken by the experience of Berlin, especially the leafy western suburbs where I was living. I tried to get some of the feel of it into this poem. Living in Berlin one thinks incessantly about the Holocaust, about violence, mass hypnosis, fear and hatred, scapegoating, political consent. One of the things I came to feel, living there, reading histories of the war and books like W. G. Sebald's *Air War and Literature* and Sven Lindqvist's *A History of Bombing,* is that we are not sufficiently horrified by the sheer extent of the butchery in the twentieth century, that the human race had found ways not to absorb it. I came to think that the second most evil thing that Hitler and the German people did, after the Holocaust, was, through the Holocaust, to keep the idea of a good war afloat. Coming back to the United States, watching how easily my own countrymen were stampeded into a war based on claims about Iraq that most informed people knew to be untrue was—and remains—a shock to me. I was also outraged by the moral and political arguments made to justify the war by the president and the war's apologists. Had they said that they were willing to be responsible for the death of thirty to a hundred thousand Iraqis, most of them innocent civilians caught in the multiple crossfires, because they knew what was good for them and had decided to sacrifice their lives, and had the American people consented to that, things would at least have been clear. Commentators in all of our media repeated the other high-minded arguments about freedom and democracy without blinking and ignored the dead. So another of my impulses was to state, to try to state plainly, the counterargument. 'Bush's War' may be too frontal. It tries to weave these things—and some others—together fairly directly. And one hopes that the stuff of poetry—the complexity of a particular tone of voice, the subterranean pull of metaphor, the feel that poetry can convey of mind alive in time—will also do their work."

JANE HIRSHFIELD was born in New York City in 1953. She is the author of six books of poetry, most recently *After* (HarperCollins and Bloodaxe, 2006). She has also written a volume of essays, *Nine Gates: Entering the Mind of Poetry* (HarperCollins, 1997), and three books collecting the poems of women poets from the past. She has received fellowships from the Guggenheim and Rockefeller foundations, the National Endowment for the Arts, and the Academy of American Poets. She has lived in northern California for more than thirty years.

Of "Critique of Pure Reason," Hirshfield writes: "This poem's opening quotation was borrowed by Kant, for his *Critique of Pure Reason,* from the second-century Greek philosopher Demonax—who watched two philosophers debating for a while, then announced to the assembled listeners, 'Gentlemen of Athens, here is one man milking a billy goat, and another catching the proceeds in a sieve.'*

"The Arabic word for 'poet'—*sha'ir*—means literally 'one who knows through feeling.' This is what I write poetry to do, and each of this poem's images, stories, and statements attempts to find some emotional and intellectual footing against the allergic response raised in me by the thought of 'pure' reason, untempered by feeling. Our human lives, our loves, our minds' productions, transport and bewilder; we hunger and rummage the past even in sleep; we tell jokes under every circumstance, even in Auschwitz. Demonax built his philosophy in no small part on the lightness of humor, especially in the matter of death, both others' and his own. At age one hundred, he became unable to care for himself, and simply stopped eating—an act of unalloyed detachment. Asked about funeral arrangements, he answered, 'Don't trouble yourselves, scent will soon summon my undertakers.' His observation brings

*Translations of Demonax slightly adapted from Fowler and Fowler, *Works of Lucian of Vamosata* (Oxford: The Clarendon Press, 1905); public domain.

death closer in one way, but pushes it back in another: the words show a person fully alive and himself, immune to death until its perimeter is crossed. When the Athenians said it would be indecent to let a beloved elder's body be devoured by dogs and birds, he replied, 'Oh, no harm in making oneself useful in death to anything that lives.' The statement— still characteristically buoyant, but not 'wit' per se—holds a courteous, practical compassion, and the knowledge that self is provisional, connected with all existence. The allegiance here, Demonax's and my poem's, is to life, its beloved, felt fullness."

DANIEL JOHNSON was born in Salem, Ohio, in 1973. His poetry is featured in the anthology *I Have My Own Song for It: Modern Poems of Ohio*. He received his MFA from Warren Wilson College and was selected twice for the Poetry Center of Chicago's Juried Reading. In 2005 he began collaborating with a filmmaker and a musician to create an illuminated text of "How to Catch a Falling Knife," his first manuscript. The project involves layering poetry over live music, a dream log, phone messages, police reports, and the found home movies of a Fuller Brush salesman from Davenport, Iowa. For more of his work, visit www.danielbjohnson.com.

Of "Do Unto Others," Johnson writes: "Sitting on the hard pews of Sunday morning, I recall getting tripped up by the mixed messages that one encounters as a child in church—those of the Old Testament and those of the New, some urging compassion, others revenge. The collision of these lessons takes center stage in my poem.

"When I began writing this piece, I imagined a pastor posing to his congregation the question 'How many rocks would you stack on your brother's chest?' The knee-jerk response of most parishioners, it seems, would be 'None.' The young speaker, though, stares head-on at his own capacity for violence. In fact, he boasts of punishing innocence. It's this meeting of viciousness and vulnerability that brings to bear the full weight of the speaker's actions on his brother and also on himself. In the end, the poem's numb refusal to say more mirrors the terseness of speech where I grew up."

RICHARD KENNEY was born in Glens Falls, New York, in 1948. He teaches at the University of Washington. His books include *The Evolution of the Flightless Bird* (Yale, 1984), *Orrery* (Atheneum, 1985), and *The Invention of the Zero* (Knopf, 1993).

Of "Gods Wrought" and "Augur Gone," Kenney writes: "I think of Ovid's Rome, or Captain Cook's Hawaii, where enervated old myths were languishing into folklore, and new ones hadn't yet repopulated the cosmic niche. When I was twenty, I thought we lived in such a place. Religion (in the forms I wanly understood, believing as I did that quarks were real and Santa Claus unreal) was surely going out with a whimper, to be succeeded by science, or something. With what horrible energy certain North American and Near Eastern species have come bounding back out of their black books—who was prepared for it? Not these poems, which are concerned with alternate fearsome futures, I fear.

"As for magnetism's interest in looking after the generating equipment, one needn't have much faith in gods to pray for their work along those lines, in coming times."

MILTON KESSLER (1930–2000) was born and raised in the Bronx and Brooklyn, New York. A high school dropout, he spent time in Van Cortland Park writing poetry, and turned to singing because, as he later wrote, "to sing was the only way through." He sang for Eleanor Roosevelt, for the Handel and Haydn Society in Boston, and was a spear carrier at the Metropolitan Opera House in New York. Later, he worked as an optician and in the garment industry. He entered the University of Buffalo at age twenty-five, graduating summa cum laude in two and a half years, and then went on to get his MA at the University of Washington, where he worked with Theodore Roethke. He taught for more than thirty years at Binghamton University and abroad in England, Israel, Belgium, and Japan. He also edited *Choice* magazine and published six volumes of poems. "Each day is still full of amazement, aloneness, danger, and gratitude," he wrote. He died one month before his seventieth birthday.

GALWAY KINNELL was born in Providence, Rhode Island, in 1927. He studied at Princeton University and the University of Rochester. His volumes of poetry include *A New Selected Poems* (Houghton Mifflin, 2000), *Imperfect Thirst* (1996), *When One Has Lived a Long Time Alone* (1990), and *Selected Poems* (1980), which received both the Pulitzer Prize and the National Book Award. He has published translations of works by Yves Bonnefroy, Yvanne Goll, François Villon, and Rainer Maria Rilke. Kinnell divides his time between Vermont and New York City, where he held the Erich Maria Remarque Chair in Creative Writing at New York University.

DAVID KIRBY was born in Baton Rouge, Louisiana, in 1944 and is currently the Robert O. Lawton Distinguished Professor of English at Florida State University in Tallahassee, where he lives with his wife, the poet Barbara Hamby. His two most recent books are *The House on Boulevard St.: New and Selected Poems* (Louisiana State University Press) and *Ultra-Talk: Johnny Cash, the Mafia, Shakespeare, Drum Music, St. Teresa of Avila, and 17 Other Colossal Topics of Conversation* (University of Georgia Press). Both books were published in 2007.

Of "Ode to the Personals," Kirby writes: "Here's a poem that illustrates the fact that most poems start with trivial beginnings, though if you allow enough time to elapse as you reconsider and revise, then the poem can grow beyond that humble start and get up on its hind legs and start walking away from you, the poet. My formula for this is B + T = P, or Beginning plus Time equals Poem. For the great works, the formula can be stated as $B + T^2 = P^2$ or Beginning plus Lots of Time equals Great Poem.

"In this case, my start was typically mingy. I've always read the personals in the *International Herald Tribune* when I've been abroad, and the people described there are more gods and goddesses than human beings: they all have two or three PhDs, own several multinational corporations, and flit constantly from one to another of the several seaside villas they own, even as they have Norman Rockwellish ambitions to settle down and enjoy a contented domestic life. What they don't seem to have is a grasp of basic English. But what the hell: the more I read these ads and thought about what kind of people might actually be behind them, the more I realized that most folks base their relationships on information that isn't a whole lot more reliable than what you get from the personals. Halfway through the poem, the speaker gets tired of sitting in his tree and decides to grab a vine and step out into the air: there's a big jungle waiting, and it's full of monkeys."

JULIE LARIOS was born in Ellensburg, Washington, in 1949 and now lives in Seattle. Last year, her work received a Pushcart Prize and was included in *The Best American Poetry 2006*. She is completing a manuscript of poems titled "A Quiet Day in the Arm and Leg Shop." Harcourt Children's Books will be publishing her fourth book for children, *Imaginary Menagerie,* in the spring of 2008.

Of "What Bee Did," Larios writes: "I like the idea of cracking words into pieces and playing with the results—it's destruction and creation all rolled into one, and that's always a thrill for a poet. For anyone, I suppose. In this poem, I cracked open words with the prefix 'be-' and the resulting root pieces began to shine and take on a foreign quality, or to sound as if they might have been used in an alehouse in the sixteenth century, where (at least to my ear) people often smirched and reaved. Then Bee was born, and after buzzing about, he luckily (I'm fond of Bee and his complicated responses to the world) made it out of the alehouse and into the dazzle."

BRAD LEITHAUSER was born in Detroit in 1953. He graduated from Harvard College and Harvard Law School. He is the author of five books of poetry, five novels, a novel in verse, two books of light verse, and a book of essays. He has received a Guggenheim Fellowship, an Ingram Merrill grant, and a MacArthur Fellowship.

Of "A Good List," Leithauser writes: "Insomnia has its costs, but perhaps the greatest is a sense of waste. All those stagnant hours—days, months, years!—when the mind is effectively painting a wall gray, or scrubbing at an indelible stain, or shoveling an icy sidewalk with a dented shovel. . . .

"So I take special pleasure in those poems born out of my chronic sleeplessness. 'A Good List' is one of these. It was written in Iceland in January, when nights are very long indeed. I was alone in a house without music—without electricity—and I began to think about the American popular song, and Lorenz Hart, who was the lyric-writing half of the Rodgers-and-Hart songwriting partnership. Hart loved outlandish rhymes, and he had his share of difficult nights. I wrote in the hope that the poem would have pleased him."

BEN LERNER was born in Topeka, Kansas, in 1979. He holds degrees in creative writing and political science from Brown University. A former Fulbright Scholar in Spain, Lerner cofounded and coedits *No: a journal of the arts* (www.nojournal.com). His first book, *The Lichtenberg Figures,* was published by Copper Canyon Press in 2004 and was named one of the best poetry books of the year by *Library Journal.* Copper Canyon published his second book, *Angle of Yaw,* in 2006. It was a finalist for the National Book Award.

Lerner writes: "There are ninety prose poems in *Angle of Yaw,* and the two printed here indicate a few of the sequence's recurrent concerns. The first poem, which appears early in the book, introduces the tragicomedy of negativity, of the Bartleby figure who refuses even refusal. The second poem is one of many in the series examining space travel as an attempt to occupy the vantage of an absent deity, to replace 'in the eyes of God' with 'visible from space,' to replace the God-term with a camera. I hope 'system of measure' is heard as referring both to our politics and our poetry.

"I should note the difficulty of composing a prose note to a series of self-referential prose poems. Is it an important characteristic of much contemporary poetry that it contains its own interpretation, that the critical supplement is incorporated into the work? See Michael Clune's essay on Kevin Davies's poetry in *No: a journal of the arts* #4, if you're interested."

JOANIE MACKOWSKI was born in Illinois in 1963, but she grew up in Connecticut, near the Long Island Sound. After earning her BA from Wesleyan University, she moved to California and worked as a journalist and a juggler. Her book of poems *The Zoo* (Pitt Poetry Series, 2002) was awarded the Kate Tufts Discovery Award. A former Wallace Stegner Fellow, she has studied literature at the University of Washington and the University of Missouri, earning an MFA and a PhD in English. She is an assistant professor at the University of Cincinnati.

Mackowski writes: " 'When I was a dinosaur' got written quickly— within a couple of weeks—which for me is unusual. At the nuts-and-bolts level, the poem began with the headstones, when I happened on a picture of a stegosaurus. Then I read about the stegosaurus: found the 'armed roof,' the seventeen plates, the two brains. The poem's built of loosely rhymed and erratically measured couplets, a device I enjoy, for I bend it and it bends me, reciprocally.

"At the level of ideas, the poem briefly explores the lyric 'I' or 'voice.' The 'I' in this poem is 1) extinct, 2) still talking, 3) something other than itself.

"And at the level of what's personal (how nice if life itself would keep to such neat categories: bolts, brains, personal: yet writing is an opportunity to play with such luxuries as logic and order), my mother has Alzheimer's, and on my mind is the extent of her experience and mental power that, because of this disease, has been misplaced. The dinosaur is not an allegory for my mother's situation, nor for the plight of any person with a brain-ravaging condition; however, my experience with how one can be simultaneously present and lost contributed to this poem's construction."

AMIT MAJMUDAR was born in New York City in 1979. He works as a diagnostic radiology resident physician in Cleveland, Ohio, where he lives with his wife. More information about him can be found at his website, http://web.mac.com/majmudar.

Of "By Accident," Majmudar writes: "On *The Price Is Right* there was a pricing game called Plinko. A huge slanted board had an array of pegs on it, evenly spaced rows evenly staggered. The contestant stood at the top and let a disk drop. The disk bumped and slid and bumped its way through that geometrical forest and ended up in one of several slots at the bottom. The slots were worth different amounts of money. One of them was the jackpot in glittery numbers.

"Like that Plinko disk's, a ghazal's slip and stumble to the bottom of the page is pretty much impossible to predict, and where it ends up may not be worth that much. (Of course it could hit the jackpot, too: That's what keeps us playing.) The formal properties of language, that mathematical component to poetry that accounts for why poets used to call verse 'numbers,' are the pegs shaping the ghazal's path: regularity rendering randomness inevitable, an obstacle course thwarting aim and will—yet giving the game all its excitement as the ghazal drops from couplet to couplet. Every end rhyme and refrain bumps the ghazal off course until its course is determined wholly by deviation, and its movement, unguessable beforehand, seems in retrospect inevitable."

SABRINA ORAH MARK was born in Mexico in 1975, and was raised in Brooklyn. She received a BA from Barnard College and an MFA from the Iowa Writers' Workshop. Her first book, *The Babies,* won the 2004 Saturnalia Books Poetry Prize (judged by Jane Miller) and was published by Saturnalia Books. Woodland Editions published her chapbook, *Walter B.'s Extraordinary Cousin Arrives for a Visit & Other Tales.* She has received fellowships from the Fine Arts Work Center in Provincetown, the Glenn Schaeffer Foundation, and the National Endowment for the Arts. She is completing a doctorate and teaching creative writing and literature at the University of Georgia.

Of "The 10 Stages of Beatrice," Mark writes: "When I wrote this poem I knew Beatrice only in stages, or as Beatrice would later say, 'she knew me only in crumbs and in morsels.' I admired Beatrice from afar as one might admire a white fur coat perched on the bow of a ship. Years later, when I was cold, Beatrice draped that white fur coat over my shoulders, and ever since that wintry day she has become whole enough to sink ten ships."

CAMPBELL MCGRATH was born in Chicago, Illinois, in 1962, and lives in Miami Beach with his wife and sons. He teaches in the MFA program at Florida International University, where he is the Philip and Patricia Frost Professor of Creative Writing. He has won MacArthur and Guggenheim fellowships, and the Kingsley Tufts Prize. His books are: *Capitalism* (Wesleyan University Press, 1990); *American Noise* (Ecco Press, 1993); *Spring Comes to Chicago* (Ecco Press, 1996); *Road Atlas* (Ecco Press, 1999); *Florida Poems* (Ecco Press, 2002); *Pax Atomica* (Ecco Press, 2004); and *Seven Notebooks,* from which "Ode to the Plantar Fascia" is taken (forthcoming from Ecco Press in 2008).

McGrath writes: " 'Ode to the Plantar Fascia' is a playful poem that punningly investigates the etymological and anatomical roots of the body politic. It pays simultaneous homage to an overlooked body part and to the historical pertinacity of language, and its conclusion is one of both empirical and imperial humility: even the humblest foot soldier may bring the empire to its knees. Creatively, the poem springs from two traditional sources: pain and language.

"To begin with the pain: after years of jogging on city streets and sandy beaches (to call it 'running' would lend it a false dignity), my feet began to ache; the ache became chronic heel and arch pain which, after a long period of denial, terminated my life as a jogger. Ouch. The culprit was plantar fasciitis, chronic inflammation of the plantar fascia, the bundle of tissue that runs along the bottom of the foot, and a variety of therapies failed to do much to heal it. Previously I'd only heard of plantar fasciitis as an injury that sidelines a couple professional basketball players each season—perhaps I was destined for an NBA career? No. Tired of standing on frozen water bottles, I gave up on my feet, and became a swimmer.

"As for language: *planta* is Latin for the sole of the foot, and *fascia,* from the Latin for 'band' or 'sash,' is used as a descriptive technical term in both anatomy and architecture. It's also a close cousin to the Latin word *fascis,* or 'bundle,' the plural of which, *fasces,* was the name given the symbol of Roman authority—a bundle of sticks wrapped around an axe traditionally carried by lictors. ('Fascism' also derives from *fascis* and the *fasces*.) Lictors were a type of official bodyguard and civil servant whose duty was to accompany consuls and other magistrates everywhere they went, and my only disappointment with the poem is my failure to work into it the word 'lictor.' "

LESLIE ADRIENNE MILLER was born in Medina, Ohio, in 1956. Her collections of poems include *The Resurrection Trade* (Graywolf Press, 2007), *Eat*

Quite Everything You See (Graywolf, 2002), *Yesterday Had a Man in It* (Carnegie Mellon University Press, 1998), *Ungodliness* (Carnegie Mellon, 1994), and *Staying Up for Love* (Carnegie Mellon, 1990). She has won a number of prizes and awards, including the Loft McKnight Award of Distinction, two Minnesota State Arts Board fellowships in poetry, a National Endowment for the Arts fellowship in poetry, and the PEN Southwest Discovery Award. She holds an MFA in poetry from the Iowa Writers' Workshop and a PhD from the University of Houston. She is a professor of English at the University of St. Thomas in St. Paul, Minnesota.

Of "On Leonardo's Drawings," Miller writes: "Initially inspired by my reading of Natalie Angier's *Woman: An Intimate Geography,* where I first discovered the rich history of medical constructions and images of the female body (in this case, Leonardo da Vinci's anatomical works and the Hippocratic corpus), I ended up writing a series of poems based on my own encounters with these visual and textual misunderstandings (*The Resurrection Trade*). Angier's book led me to more detailed histories of art, anatomy, and midwifery in Europe from the medieval period through the nineteenth century, where I found fascinating (hilarious, gorgeous, grotesque, and just plain sad) anatomical images of women hidden away in medical books. As I exercised my curiosity about these drawings and the women who inhabited them, I found gross (in both senses of the word) misunderstandings of female anatomy that persisted well into the twentieth century, and the seeds of these misunderstandings still reside in contemporary cultural constructions of women. As the productions of working fine artists, antique medical drawings say something about art; as the tools of medical professionals, they say something about how we came to understand the physicality of the female body; as images which necessarily were almost always accompanied by text, they also have much to say about language. Revisiting these images and text in and out of their original contexts allowed me to look again at how science and art have been coconspirators in the construction of gender in the West. In 'On Leonardo's Drawings' I mean to share both my amusement and horror, to offer a way in under the skin, and to encourage readers to rethink their own idiosyncratic bodies of knowledge."

MARILYN NELSON was born in Cleveland, Ohio, in 1946, and grew up on military bases in the United States. She holds a BA from the University of California, Davis, an MA from the University of Pennsylvania, and a PhD from the University of Minnesota. Her major publications are *For the Body* (1978), *Mama's Promises* (1985), *The Homeplace* (1990), *Magnifi-*

cat (1994), *The Fields of Praise: New and Selected Poems* (1997), and *The Cachoiera Tales and Other Poems* (2005), all published by the Louisiana State University Press; *Carver: A Life in Poems* (2001), and *Fortune's Bones: The Manumission Requiem* (2005), published by Front Street Books; and *A Wreath for Emmett Till* (2005), published by Houghton Mifflin. She has translated Euripides (*Hecuba*) and the Danish poets Halfdan Rasmussen and Inge Pedersen. She served as Poet Laureate of the state of Connecticut from 2001 to 2006.

Of "Etymology," Nelson writes: "This sonnet is part of a sequence of twelve that will soon be published (by Front Street Books) with a sequence of twelve sonnets by Elizabeth Alexander on the same subject: the short-lived boarding school for 'young ladies and little misses of color' opened by Miss Prudence Crandall in the village of Canterbury, Connecticut, in 1833.

"Teacher and students were harassed; a law was passed to ban the school; Crandall was arrested and jailed; the well was poisoned; the house set on fire. This sonnet imagines a student who is a born scholar, a genius interested in the history of languages. It is 1833; elsewhere in this nation girls like her were enslaved. But the scene she describes might be taken from my memories of the television news in the 1950s, or from one of my own experiences as a child, or during the summer months I spent working for the civil rights movement in Chicago when Dr. King brought the movement north.

"The girl in the poem is horrified, but she also feels the intellectual's scientific curiosity."

ED OCHESTER was born in Brooklyn, New York, in 1939. He has been the editor of the University of Pittsburgh Press Poetry Series since 1978, and is a core faculty member of the Bennington MFA Writing Seminars. His most recent books, all published in 2007, are *The Republic of Lies,* a chapbook from Adastra Press; *Unreconstructed: New & Selected Poems* (Autumn House Press); and *American Poetry Now* (University of Pittsburgh Press), an anthology of contemporary work.

Ochester writes: " 'Voltaire at Cirey, 1736' was written after I had read Nancy Mitford's biography *Voltaire in Love,* and reflects my long-standing affection (since high school!) for Voltaire. People say again and again that Americans pay no attention to or despise 'history,' and in some ways that seems to be a pretty accurate generalization. But I enjoy reading history, and have found that—time and time again—such reading leads to poems, though rarely to poems which make as overt a comparison between two time periods as this one does."

MEGHAN O'ROURKE was born in New York City in 1976. She is the literary editor of *Slate* and a poetry editor at *The Paris Review*, and her poems and essays have appeared in *The New Yorker, The New Republic, Poetry, The Kenyon Review*, and other venues. Her first book of poems, *Halflife*, was published by W. W. Norton in 2007. She has lived in Brooklyn most of her life.

Of "Peep Show," O'Rourke writes: "My poems are often stitched together out of disconnected observations, and what I say afterward about them usually seems false to me—as if it wants to take the place of the random concentration that went into the poem's making. But I wrote this poem in the summer of 2002 in a borrowed room overlooking the sea. It had a widow's walk stretching out past the window, and I spent most of my time there just watching the water and not writing. During that period, I was thinking a lot about the degree to which public spectacle shaped individual experience, and what that meant to the imagination. And I was reading Walt Whitman and Baudelaire, enamored of both Baudelaire's lyrical compression and Whitman's expansive scope. 'Peep Show' was an attempt to have it both ways. I suppose brevity won."

GREGORY ORR was born in Albany, New York, in 1947. He is the author of nine collections of poetry, the most recent of which is *Concerning the Book That Is the Body of the Beloved* (Copper Canyon Press, 2005). Among his other poetry books are *The Caged Owl: New and Selected Poems* (Copper Canyon Press, 2002), *Orpheus and Eurydice, City of Salt We Must Make a Kingdom of It, The Red House, Gathering the Bones Together,* and *Burning the Empty Nests.* He has also written a memoir, *The Blessing* (Council Oak Books, 2002), and a book on the existential function of the personal lyric, *Poetry as Survival* (University of Georgia Press, 2002). He is a professor of English at the University of Virginia, where he has taught since 1975. He founded and was the first director of the university's MFA program in writing. He lives with his wife, the painter Trisha Orr, and his two daughters in Charlottesville, Virginia.

Of "Weeping, weeping, weeping . . . ," Orr writes: "This poem is one of 180 untitled poems that make up a lyric sequence entitled *Concerning the Book That Is the Body of the Beloved,* which was published in book form by Copper Canyon Press in 2005. The sequence began when I woke up one morning with the following phrase in my head: 'the Book that is the resurrection of the body of the beloved, which is the world.' That phrase was too long to fit on a book cover, but the poems of the sequence unfolded from it—an exploration of its implications and permutations. The 'Book' is an (imagined, almost infinite) anthology that contains all lyric poems and songs ever written. We continually pull poems from it for consolation, celebration, or illumination (making our own, personal, smaller versions of it). The beloved is (in Sappho's phrase) 'whatever one loves most,' and is a figure constantly lost to us, constantly restored/resurrected through lyric poetry."

DANIELLE PAFUNDA was born in Albany, New York, in 1977. She is the author of *Pretty Young Thing* (Soft Skull Press, 2005) and *A Primer for Cyborgs: The Corpse* (Whole Coconut Chapbook Series, 2007). *My Zorba* is forthcoming from Bloof Books in 2008. Her work appears in previous editions of *Best American Poetry,* journals such as *Conjunctions, TriQuarterly,* and *jubilat,* and the anthology *Not for Mothers Only* (Fence Books, 2007). She is coeditor of the online journal *La Petite Zine* and is about to launch the micropress Wunderbin Books. She is completing her doctorate in creative writing at the University of Georgia.

Of "Dear Pearce & Pearce, Inc.," Pafunda writes: "My second manuscript, *My Zorba,* a *Mommie Dearest*–meets–Ziggy Stardust gender bender, contains the epistolary series 'In the Iron Caisson.' After much tumult, 'I' locks 'Zorba' in the basement, and proceeds to send hurried communications to concerned parties—Aunt Hemorrhage and Uncle Rottweiler, an elementary school classroom, Dr. Jawbones, and Pearce & Pearce, Inc., to name a few. Some of the addressees could be said to exist in the real world. Some could be said to supply a sort of health insurance to the graduate student population of the real world's universities."

CHAD PARMENTER was born in Sacramento, California, in 1977 and is currently enrolled in the doctoral program in creative writing at the University of Missouri–Columbia. His work has appeared in such journals as *The Harvard Review, Smartish Pace,* and *Hotel Amerika.*

Of "A Tech's Ode to the Genome Computer," Parmenter writes: "In this poem, I was exploring my fears around the human genome project, which holds vast implications for the history of humanity and of the planet. The idea of the human as text, and fundamentally knowable as such, speaks to the genome project, to the poem itself, and to the confrontation of otherness that for me is intertwined with the plunge into love. Also, it's a poem about needing to remain mysterious, and to be known, and the point at which the first is decoded to show the second glowing at its core."

SUSAN PARR was born in Las Cruces, New Mexico, in 1967, of Wisconsin parents. She grew up in several states, residing longest in Florida. She earned a BA in Russian studies from Barnard College and an MFA in poetry from the University of Washington. She has lived in Seattle since the early 1990s. "Swooping Actuarial Fauna" and "Ecstatic Cling" are her first published poems. Her illustrations have appeared in the *Portlandia Review of Books*.

Of "Swooping Actuarial Fauna," Parr writes: "The poem tells what the fauna are and tells where they go. Telling where they go comes first. It's a poem that probably wants to be a found poem, but is made— of nouns and verbs and other parts I found scattered in a word list attached to unsolicited e-mail sent me by Renegade K. Leveraged, or someone of her ilk. Made, that is, of subfragments—sent by a figment."

Of "Ecstatic Cling," Parr writes: "There was biting in my life, circa 1974, but not the bite of an electrician's boy. It was a girl, biting—and a girl, bitten—and I was biter, not bitten. But much energy is gained from making a 'having been bitten' from a bite. What actually required less effort was the exchange in my imagination of girl for boy, whence came the bodies behind those teeth and thumbs. The last line of the poem was won in an early morning struggle, not unlike the scene described, except I was the only one there."

PETER PEREIRA was born in Spokane, Washington, in 1959. He attended the University of Washington School of Medicine, and practices as a family physician in Seattle. His books include *What's Written on the Body* (Copper Canyon, 2007), *Saying the World* (Copper Canyon, 2003), and *The Lost Twin* (Grey Spider, 2000). He was a winner of the 2005 Glenna Luschei Prize from *Prairie Schooner* and a 1997 "Discovery"/*The Nation* Award. This is his first appearance in *The Best American Poetry*.

Pereira writes: "Medicine is full of wonderful eponyms. The term 'Nursemaid's Elbow' (also known as radial head subluxation) harkens back to the days when a nursemaid or nanny was not a rarity. This poem arose from an experience a good friend and her daughter had, and the mixture of chagrin and guilt the mother recounted to me at the insinuation inherent in the common name for her daughter's injury. I endeavor to write medical poems that can encapsulate a clinical situation, or dramatize a clinical pearl. This one just happened to evolve to sonnet size, with a hint of a nursery-rhyme melody. It would give me great joy if a medical student, resident, or attending physician were one day to be reminded how to diagnose and treat a case of Nursemaid's Elbow simply by having this little poem in memory. Or if a mother (or other parent or caregiver) could read this poem and have comfort knowing that her doctors, when they use this term, are not meaning to judge her."

ROBERT PINSKY was born in 1940 in Long Branch, New Jersey. His new book of poetry is *Gulf Music* (Farrar Straus and Giroux, 2007). He is also the author of *The Life of David* (Schocken/Nextbook), a prose work published in 2005, and editor of *An Invitation to Poetry* (Norton, 2004), an anthology and DVD based on the Favorite Poem Project. His best-selling translation, *The Inferno of Dante,* won the *Los Angeles Times* Book Award in poetry. He has appeared as a regular on *The NewsHour with Jim Lehrer* and writes the weekly "Poet's Choice" column for the *Washington Post Book World.* He teaches in the graduate writing program at Boston University.

Of "Louie Louie," Pinsky writes: "Forgetting is never perfect, just as recall is never total: the memorized poem or phone number may be recalled, but never with the exact feeling it had. And conversely, forgotten details may be obliterated, but a feeling lingers on.

"The trite notion that Americans lack memory or historical awareness is unsatisfying. *How* might we lack it, severally and collectively? One doesn't need Freud to understand that both memory and forgetting are willful and involuntary, helpless and desperate, in mysterious measures. Forgetting is not mere absence. Everything is partly a ruin, and the ruin is haunted.

"In the haunted ruin of my consciousness, or of my country, one of the mad voices is the journalism that swallows and regurgitates as it speaks the clutter of what I have heard of or not heard of—or what I have merely heard of, and no more. Sometimes from the babble a kind of clarity emerges, a genius: great comics of the early twentieth century say the greatest of them was Bert Williams. I have heard him, and he is an angel of comic song. He is partly forgotten—partly because he was a black man, and partly because he found he could do his best work only in blackface.

"In early drafts, 'Louie Louie' was called 'Heard' and 'Forgetting' and

'I Never Heard Of.' A close friend was mystified: how I could claim I had never heard of George W. Bush. What could I answer? That I liked saying I had not heard of him? That there was a time not long ago when we had not heard of him—a failed oilman rich-boy-son fronting for a baseball team? That someday someone, indeed many people, will not have heard of him? That the poem was meant to be in part an irritable and irritating babble?

"And how can the poem name so many things it hasn't heard of? Because it is acting dumb, I suppose, in a smart-ass way involving the contradiction or paradox of naming what one has never heard of— clearly the name must have been heard at least once by whoever says 'I never heard of it.'

"The same friend, when he later came to accept the poem (in a later draft), suggested naming it after the magnetic song by Richard Berry recorded by the Kingsmen. The song is an amazing thing; we have heard it, and we have heard of it. FBI agents investigated it and hallucinated a subversive understanding of its hard-to-understand words.

" 'Stupid Meditation on Peace' was commissioned by the Manhae Foundation, a Korean Buddhist organization, as part of a World Festival of Peace, with ceremonies in both North and South Korea. Appreciative of the honor, respectful of my hosts, I also wanted to include my own deficiencies of peace: thus the Hopkins quotation about cooing; the shit-throwing; the word 'stupid'; the traditional Buddhist 'monkey-mind.' The idea of two contrasting tributary streams, Peace and Art, comes from a passage in the autobiography of Sid Caesar."

DAVID RIVARD was born in Fall River, Massachusetts, in 1953. He is the author of four books of poems: *Sugartown* (Graywolf, 2006); *Bewitched Playground* (Graywolf, 2000); *Wise Poison* (Graywolf, 1996), winner of the James Laughlin Prize from the Academy of American Poets; and *Torque* (University of Pittsburgh Press, 1988), winner of the Agnes Lynch Starrett Prize. He was recently awarded the 2006 O. B. Hardison, Jr. Poetry Prize from the Folger Shakespeare Library. He has received fellowships from the Guggenheim Foundation, the National Endowment for the Arts, and the Fine Arts Work Center in Provincetown. He teaches at Tufts University.

Rivard writes: " 'The Rev. Larry Love Is Dead' was one of the earliest poems written for my most recent book, *Sugartown*. Formally, I was interested in collaging together a set of image fragments, floating them along a line of highly enjambed syntax. I also wanted to have rhythmic resistances, catches, pauses to counterpoint the flow of the speech. The sound of the place where Issa meets George Oppen, if you will. The refrain in the first half of the poem is adapted from W. C. Williams.

"There was an actual Rev. Larry Love, a street character in Cambridge. Born Lawrence Hinkson, he had a minor hit in the 1950s with a doo-wop band called the Lovenotes. In the early 1990s, he would roller-skate between Harvard and Central Square, dressed in leg warmers, an orange crossing guard's vest or drum major's jacket, a police hat, and sometimes (in my mind's eye, anyway) shorts and twirling a baton. Comically charming, cosmic, and flirtatious, but with enough crankiness in him to guarantee that he was nobody's clown. He passed in 2001, a native of the old Cambridge (and a citizen of 'the old, weird America,' as Greil Marcus would say), a stranger in the culture of gentrified amnesia."

MARYA ROSENBERG was born in New York City in 1985, and grew up in Manhattan. She was accepted at the United States Military Academy at West Point in 2003 and entered cadet basic training that June, two days after she graduated from high school.

Rosenberg writes: "I've had a lot of interesting experiences at West Point: I've gotten to shoot a 50-caliber machine gun, throw hand grenades, jump out of airplanes (I graduated from airborne school last summer), break a few bones, date an assortment of wildly inappropriate guys, and spend a fair amount of time crawling around in the mud, being miserable. At the moment, I'm in my senior year at the academy, and I hope to graduate in May 2007 with a degree in English and a commission as a second lieutenant. I'm going to be in the Adjutant General's Corps, and I'm hoping to be stationed in Korea for my first year in the army. I have to serve at least five years on active duty after graduation, and I'm thinking of making the army a career. Eventually, I would like to become either an army lawyer or a specialist in East Asian affairs. The poem included in this anthology, as well as one other, were originally published in the Fall 2006 issue of *Hanging Loose*. That was my first publication, and my only one to date.

"My father has been reading haiku to me since I was a small child, and I wrote a few haiku of my own for the first time in elementary school. However, I didn't start to work seriously on writing poetry until my first year at West Point, when my freshman English teacher, LTC Robert Gibson, encouraged me to do so. Since then, I've written a great many haiku, mostly about West Point, since I think the haiku form is particularly well suited to descriptions of the academy's many absurdities and charms. All of the haiku in this series are based, at least loosely, on real experiences I've had here and people I've known."

NATASHA SAJÉ was born in Munich, Germany, in 1955, and earned degrees from the University of Virginia, Johns Hopkins, and the University of Maryland. She is the author of two books of poems, *Red Under the Skin* (Pittsburgh, 1994) and *Bend* (Tupelo Press, 2004), and many essays. She has received the Robert Winner Award, the Campbell Corner Poetry Prize, the Utah Book Award, and a Fulbright Fellowship. Sajé is an associate professor of English at Westminster College in Salt Lake City, and has been teaching in the Vermont College low-residency MFA program since 1996.

Of "F," Sajé writes: "For the poems in this series, I start by listing evocative words that contain a specific English letter (I've also used letters from other alphabets, for instance š in Slovenian), after which I choose words that cohere and try to devise a question around them. As a poem takes shape, I devise a form for it. Some of these abecedarian poems are prose, others are sonnets or pantoums, but most are unique forms. One pleasure comes from seeing the poem channel my (previously) unconscious concerns; another pleasure is fooling around with tone and form. With 'F' I enjoyed changing 'firethorn' to its other name, 'bittersweet,' at the end of the poem, and making the last line begin with 'passed.'"

FREDERICK SEIDEL was born in St. Louis, Missouri, in 1936. He attended Harvard College. Three of his recent books of poems—*The Cosmos Poems* (2001), *Life on Earth* (2001), and *Area Code 212* (2002)—were published in a single volume, *The Cosmos Trilogy,* in 2003. His latest collection is *Ooga-Booga* (2006). Since 1993 he has been published by Farrar, Straus and Giroux.

ALAN SHAPIRO was born in Boston, Massachusetts, in 1952. He is the William R. Kenan Jr. Distinguished Professor of English at the University of North Carolina at Chapel Hill. His most recent book, *Tantalus in Love,* was published in 2005 by Houghton Mifflin, which will publish his new book, *From the Book of Last Thoughts,* in 2008.

Shapiro writes: " 'Country Western Singer' is from the title sequence of my next book, *from the Book of Last Thoughts,* which attempts to imagine the last thoughts (not the last words) of a variety of characters and speakers (everyone from the president to the pronoun 'I'). The title of each poem identifies the speaker. For each speaker, I choose a different verse form and idiom expressive of his or her or its particular character and situation. In this poem, written as a song, or ballad, a country western singer is dying of alcohol poisoning. It's meant to be a profoundly affectionate parody of a genre of music I love."

DAVID SHUMATE was born in Iowa City, Iowa, in 1950. His first book of prose poems, *High Water Mark* (University of Pittsburgh Press, 2004), was awarded the Agnes Lynch Starrett Prize. He lives in Zionsville, Indiana, and teaches at Marian College in Indianapolis.

Of "Drawing Jesus," Shumate writes: "We were driving from New Mexico to Indiana, somewhere east of Goodland, Kansas. I remember it quite clearly. It was the night of the July full moon, 2005. I asked Carol if she would jot down a note: 'Drawing Jesus.' That's all I had at the time: a title. As she was writing, I said, 'If I can't make something out of that, I'd better just close up shop.'"

CARMINE STARNINO was born in Montreal, Quebec, in 1970. He is the author of three books of poetry: *The New World* (Signal Editions, 1997), *Credo* (McGill–Queen's University Press, 2000), and *With English Subtitles* (Gaspereau, 2004). A collection of essays on Canadian poetry, *A Lover's Quarrel,* was published by the Porcupine's Quill in 2005. Starnino has also edited *The New Canon: An Anthology of Canadian Poetry* (Signal Editions, 2005). He has received the Canadian Authors Association Prize, the A. M. Klein Prize for Poetry, and the F. G. Bressani Prize. He is an associate editor at *Maisonneuve.*

Starnino writes: "I started 'Money' on a visit to London in 1998 and finally finished it in 2003 while attending the Château de Lavigny retreat in Switzerland. Inspirations for the poem were a visit to the British Museum, Wallace Stevens's notion that 'Money is a kind of poetry,' and my father's tendency—which I've since picked up—of playing with the change in his pockets while waiting in line. What did spending six years on the poem teach me? That Voltaire was absolutely right. 'It is easier to write about money than to acquire it.'"

BRIAN TURNER was born in Visalia, California, in 1967. He earned an MFA from the University of Oregon and lived abroad in South Korea for a year before serving for seven years in the U.S. Army. He was an infantry team leader for a year in Iraq beginning November 2003, with the 3rd Stryker Brigade Combat Team, 2nd Infantry Division. Earlier, he was deployed to Bosnia-Herzegovina in 1999–2000 with the 10th Mountain Division. His poetry has been published in *Poetry Daily* and *The Georgia Review*, and in the *Voices in Wartime* anthology published in conjunction with the feature-length documentary film of the same name. He received a 2007 National Endowment for the Arts Literature Fellowship in Poetry.

Of "What Every Soldier Should Know," Turner writes: "Prior to deploying to Iraq, my battalion gathered together in a large theater to listen to an Iraqi national offer advice and insights into Iraqi culture and customs. Of course, while in Iraq itself we learned much beyond what we initially learned that day. One of the many sad and difficult things about war is that we learn too much of what people should never know (and not enough of what we need to know)."

ARTHUR VOGELSANG was born in Baltimore, Maryland, in 1942, and has lived there and in New York City, Iowa City, Wichita, Philadelphia, Paris, Las Vegas, and Los Angeles. He has been employed variously as a teacher (University of Redlands, University of Southern California, University of Nevada, Wichita State University, the Kansas Arts Commission, University of Iowa) and as an editor (*The American Poetry Review*, 1973–2006). His books of poetry are *A Planet* (Holt, 1983), *Twentieth Century Women* (University of Georgia Press, 1988), *Cities and Towns* (University of Massachusetts Press, 1996), and *Left Wing of a Bird* (Sarabande, 2003). He has traveled extensively in Mexico, Florida, and Delaware.

Vogelsang writes: " 'The Family' is the first poem in a sequence ('The Family II,' 'Mother's First Airplane,' 'Komodo,' and 'Yes' are the others) which deals with people in communities as small as two persons, through to the larger arrangements of neighborhoods, countries, and continents, and what we may imagine in our search to reach beyond those around us. The five poems have appeared together in the *Colorado Review*. Unavoidably, as may be inevitable with most poetry, the poems comment upon the nature of human beings and, also unavoidably, upon the nature of animals. Peripherally (or perhaps not) I'd like to note that there are more people alive than all the people dead, and, as to be expected, more animals dead than all the animals alive, including insects in these tallies."

CODY WALKER was born in Baltimore, Maryland, in 1967. He now lives in Seattle, where he serves as a writer-in-residence at the Richard Hugo House.

Walker writes: " 'Coulrophobia' owes its existence to Arnost Lustig (in whose comedic presence the piece was first conceived) and its last lines to Richard Kenney. As the narrator might say, God bless both of them."

KARY WAYSON was born in 1970 in Hanover, New Hampshire, but grew up mainly in Portland, Oregon. She received the 2003 "Discovery"/*The Nation* award and a 2001 Artist Trust/Washington State Arts Commission Fellowship. Her poems have appeared in *Poetry Northwest, The Nation,* and *FIELD. Dog & Me,* a chapbook, was published by LitRag Press in 2004. She teaches poetry writing for the Richard Hugo House in Seattle, Washington.

Wayson writes: "Like most poets I'm often asked the question 'What do you write about?' I have yet to prepare a reasonable reply. I did not set out to write 'Flu Song in Spanish' as a poem *about* a thing or a feeling. What happened was that I wrote the line 'I stuck my head in a hole and stood' and then got 'Now I wear that hole like a hood' from the image and the rhyme of the first line. After I transferred those two lines from notebook to notebook, they became the mechanism of the engine of the finished poem, which took at least six months to make once I got started in earnest. The title, 'Flu Song in Spanish,' articulates (rather than explains) the mystery of the poem, which I built more out of sound and rhythm than out of an intention toward particular meaning. Also, and maybe most plainly, the title is a way of trying to let myself off the hook: No, I did not just call my father a bitch—and if I did, then I don't remember—I must have been crazy with fever and speaking in a language I've never learned."

CHARLES HARPER WEBB was born in Philadelphia, Pennsylvania, in 1952, and grew up in Houston, Texas. His book of prose poems, *Hot Popsicles,* was published by University of Wisconsin Press in 2005, and his fifth book of verse, *Amplified Dog,* by Red Hen Press in 2006. He has received the Morse, Pollock, and Saltman prizes, the Kate Tufts Discovery Award, a Whiting Writers' Award, and a Guggenheim Fellowship. A former rock singer, guitarist, and psychotherapist, Webb edited *Stand Up Poetry: An Expanded Anthology* (University of Iowa, 2002), and directs the creative writing program at California State University, Long Beach.

Webb writes: "I wish I could say that the idea for 'Big' came after I was crowned Mr. Universe, or was asked to star in my own porno series (I refused), or even looked at my paycheck for the month. But no, the poem began the day I bought a big TV. I don't mean just a big screen; I mean a TV so enormous it took four straining men to lift it from my truck, and five to wrestle it into my home. The poem is literally true. Even the surfing part. (I couldn't size the California waves from shore or as I paddled out, glasses left safely in my car. I almost died.) The Big One may level Los Angeles someday. But that TV will remain— unmoved, immovable—when Gibraltar is dust."

JOE WENDEROTH was born in Baltimore, Maryland, in 1966. Wesleyan University Press published his first two books of poetry, *Disfortune* (1995) and *It Is If I Speak* (2000). *Letters to Wendy's,* a novel in verse, and *The Holy Spirit of Life: Essays Written for John Ashcroft's Secret Self,* were published by Verse Press in 2000 and 2005, respectively. *No Real Light,* a book of poems, is forthcoming from Wave Books in 2007, and *Agony: A Proposal,* a work of fiction, will be published by either Wave Books or Riverhead (or both). Wenderoth teaches at the University of California, Davis.

Of "The Home of the Brave," Wenderoth writes: "This poem is unusual, from my perspective, for two reasons. First, it's topical, which my poems tend very much not to be. I saw the Nick Berg decapitation video online, and I felt compelled to write a poem about it. Second, it's to some degree political; my political thoughts and feelings don't usually overlap with the thoughts and feelings that poems stem from or tend to. As unusual as the poem is, however, I suspect its core is quite typically poetic. I'd agree with Allen Grossman that poems always originate in some disruption of the autonomy of the will, and the video, a ritual sacrifice, is a conspicuous instance of just that phenomenon. The autonomy of Nick Berg's will is obviously disrupted, but so is the autonomy of the will of the viewer—in this case, me. This placed me in an odd situation. That is, while I was provided with one small but decisive glimpse into the ongoing horrors caused by U.S. foreign policy, I was at the same time made to feel that it was not at all in my power to make these horrors cease. The poem I wrote manifests the struggle to keep these contradictory forces intact; if the poem works, it makes the hearer feel both the potency and the impotency of the will he thinks of as his own."

RICHARD WILBUR was born in New York City in 1921. A graduate of Amherst College, he served with the 36th Infantry Division in World War II. After teaching at Harvard, Wellesley, Wesleyan, and Smith, he has now retired to write. His *Collected Poems 1943–2004* was published by

Harcourt, which more recently has issued his translation of Pierre Corneille's *Theatre of Illusion* (*L'Illusion comique*). He is currently at work on another Corneille play, *The Liar.*

Wilbur writes: "My 'Opposites' poems are in the blithe sprit of the dinner-table games that my wife and I used to play with our young children. They address the child's (or adult's) desire for logical order in the world, and his suspicion that there is no such thing. I have always felt that the best 'children's verse' is not patronizing, and is capable of being enjoyed by children and grown-ups alike and together. Some children's book editors might shy at words like 'whereas' and 'deftly,' but I have heard no complaints about 'hard words' from the young."

GEORGE WITTE was born in Summit, New Jersey, in 1960, and grew up in the state's suburbs and rural northwest corner. For twenty-three years he has worked at St. Martin's Press, editing fiction and nonfiction books across a range of genres and subjects. His first collection, *The Apparitioners,* was published in 2005 by Three Rail Press.

Of "At Dusk, the Catbird," Witte writes: "Most of us have experienced what this poem describes: time slows down, and we are able to see what otherwise would vanish in a blur. I recently read a testy exchange in *Poetry* in which several poets debated the 'use' of poetry, what purpose it might serve in an indifferent world, and whether that purpose ought to be political in order for a given poem to be noticed. While the question of usefulness is too big to answer in one way or with one kind of poem, surely one function of poetry is to notice, to attend, to witness and not to turn away, and to render in language what we miss every second of the day, despite (and because of) our array of senses."

THEODORE WOROZBYT was born in Columbus, Georgia, in 1960. *The Dauber Wings* won the American Poetry Journal Book Prize and was published in 2006 by Dream Horse Press. *Scar Letters* is forthcoming from Beard of Bees Press in 2007. He teaches at the University of Alabama.

Of "An Experiment," Worozbyt writes: "I wrote this poem ten years ago and have no memory of composing it, but reading it now and thinking about the story of Lavoisier I am struck as I always am by the hideous irrationality of capital punishment, and by how little it has to do with justice and how much with the frisson of public spectacle. In the case of Lavoisier, the execution was explicitly political. But it seems to me that all executions are politically stained, whether it's a matter of not being able to afford salvation through savvy counsel, or that of a presidential pretender endorsing the cell-phone-wielding mob of a provisional government."

HARRIET ZINNES was born in Hyde Park, Massachusetts, in 1919. She was educated at Hunter College (BA, 1939), Brooklyn College (MA, 1944), and New York University (PhD, 1953). She married Irving I. Zinnes, a professor of theoretical physics, in 1943. After working as an associate editor at *Harper's Bazaar* for three years, she began teaching at Hunter College in 1946. She became a professor of English at Queens College in 1978. Her recent books include *Whither Nonstopping* (Marsh Hawk Press, 2005), *Drawing on the Wall* (Marsh Hawk Press, 2002), and *Pliunge* (Wild Honey Press , 2001). Among her other books are two collections of stories, *The Radiant Absurdity of Desire* (Avisson Press, 1998) and *Lover* (Coffee House Press, 1988) and a translation of Jacques Prévert's selected poems, *Blood and Feathers: Selected Poems of Jacques Prévert* (Asphodel Press and Moyer Bell, 1993).

Zinnes writes: "What is becomes what was. But the 'isness' remains in the memory and turns to something more stark, more identifiable not of memory but of a stark reality as if what is remembered turns in the earth slowly into a form true and real."

MAGAZINES WHERE THE POEMS
WERE FIRST PUBLISHED

Alaska Quarterly Review, ed. Ronald Spatz; guest ed. for 2006 Olena Kaly-tiak Davis. University of Alaska, 3211 Providence Dr., Anchorage, AK 99508.

American Poet, ed. Dan Brady. Academy of American Poets. www.poets.org/ampo.

The American Poetry Review, eds. Stephen Berg, David Bonanno, and Elizabeth Scanlon. 117 South 17th St., Suite 910, Philadelphia, PA 19103.

The Antioch Review, poetry ed. Judith Hall. PO Box 148, Yellow Springs, OH 45387.

Atlanta Review, ed. Dan Veach. PO Box 8248, Atlanta, GA 31106.

Barrow Street, eds. Patricia Carlin, Peter Covino, Lois Hirshkowitz, and Melissa Hotchkiss. PO Box 1831, New York, NY 10156.

Beloit Poetry Journal, eds. John Rosenwald and Lee Sharkey. PO Box 151, Farmington, ME 04938.

BOMB, ed. Betsy Sussler. 80 Hanson Pl., Suite 703, Brooklyn, NY 11217.

Bookforum, ed, Eric Banks. 350 Seventh Ave., New York, NY 10001.

Colorado Review, poetry eds. Jorie Graham and Donald Revell. Depart-ment of English, Colorado State University, Fort Collins, CO 80523.

Conduit, ed. William D. Waltz. 510 8th Ave. Northeast, Minneapolis, MN 55413.

The Cortland Review, poetry eds. Scott Challener, Jennifer Wallace, and Jennifer Wheelock. www.cortlandreview.com

Crazyhorse, poetry eds. Carol Ann Davis and Garrett Doherty. Depart-ment of English, College of Charleston, 66 George St., Charleston, SC 29424.

Denver Quarterly, ed. Bin Ramke. University of Denver, Department of English, 2000 E. Asbury, Denver, CO 80208.

Fence, poetry eds. Anthony Hawley, Katy Lederer, Christopher Stack-house, and Max Winter. 303 East 8th St., #B1, New York, NY 10009.

FIELD, eds. Pamela Alexander, Martha Collins, David Walker, and David Young. Oberlin College Press, 50 N. Professor St., Oberlin, OH 44074-1091.

Five Points, poetry eds. David Bottoms, Megan Sexton, and Beth Gylys. Georgia State University, PO Box 3999, Atlanta, GA 30302-3999.

Gulf Coast, poetry eds. Jericho Brown, Paul Otremba, and Bradford Gray Telford. Department of English, University of Houston, Houston, TX 77204-3013.

Hanging Loose, eds. Robert Hershon, Dick Lourie, and Mark Pawlak. 231 Wyckoff St., Brooklyn, NY 11217.

Iowa Review, ed. David Hamilton. 308 EPB, The University of Iowa, Iowa City, IA 52242.

The Kenyon Review, poetry ed. David Baker. www.kenyonreview.org

Literary Imagination, poetry eds. Marilyn Hacker and Reginald Shepherd. ALSC, 650 Beacon St., Suite 510, Boston, MA 02215.

Michigan Quarterly Review, ed. Laurence Goldstein. 3574 Rackham Bldg., 915 East Washington St., Ann Arbor, MI 48109-1070.

New American Writing, eds. Maxine Chernoff and Paul Hoover. 369 Molino Ave., Mill Valley, CA 94941.

The New Criterion, poetry ed. David Yezzi. 900 Broadway, Suite 602, New York, NY 10003.

New England Review, poetry ed. C. Dale Young. Middlebury College, Middlebury, VT 05753.

New Letters, ed. Robert Stewart. UMKC University House, 5101 Rockhill Rd., Kansas City, MO 64110-2499.

The New Yorker, poetry ed. Alice Quinn. 4 Times Square, New York, NY 10036.

Ploughshares, poetry ed. David Daniel. Emerson College, 120 Boylston St., Boston, MA 02116-4624.

Poet Lore, executive eds. Jody Bolz, Rick Cannon, and E. Ethelbert Miller. The Writer's Center, 4508 Walsh St., Bethesda, MD 20815.

Poetry, ed. Christian Wiman. 1030 North Clark St., Suite 420, Chicago, IL 60610.

POOL: A Journal of Poetry, eds. Patty Seyburn and Judith Taylor. PO Box 49738, Los Angeles, CA 90049.

Raritan, ed.-in-chief Jackson Lears. 31 Mine St., New Brunswick, NJ 08903.

Rattle, ed.-in-chief Alan Fox. 12411 Ventura Blvd., Studio City, CA 91604.

Sacramento News & Review, poetry ed. Kel Munger. 1015 20th St., Sacramento, CA 95814.

Sentence, ed. Brian Clements. Firewheel Editions, Box 7, Western Connecticut State University, 181 White St., Danbury, CT 06810.

Southwest Review, poetry ed. Willard Spiegelman. Southern Methodist University, Dallas, TX 75275.

Subtropics, poetry ed. Sidney Wade. PO Box 112075, 4008 Turlington Hall, University of Florida, Gainesville, FL 32611-2075.

Tarpaulin Sky, poetry eds. Christian Peet, Eireene Nealand, Julianna Spallholz, Elena Georgiou, and Lizzie Harris. PO Box 190, Saxtons River, VT 05154. www.tarpaulinsky.com

the tiny, eds. Gina Meyers and Gabriella Torres. www.thetinyjournal.com

TriQuarterly, ed. Susan Firestone Hahn. 629 Noyes St., Evanston, IL 60208-4302.

Verse, eds. Brian Henry and Andrew Zawacki. English Department, University of Richmond, Richmond, VA 23173.

Verse Daily, eds. Hunter Hamilton and Campbell Russo. www.versedaily.com

Virginia Quarterly Review, ed. Ted Genoways, poetry chair David Lee Rubin. The University of Virginia, One West Range, Box 400223, Charlottesville, VA 22904-4223.

The Vocabula Review, ed. Robert Hartwell Fiske. www.vocabula.com

ACKNOWLEDGMENTS

The series editor wishes to thank Mark Bibbins for his invaluable assistance. John Ashbery, Amy Donow, Steven Dube, Stacey Harwood, Sarah Ruth Jacobs, Deborah Landau, Kathleen Ossip, and Michael Schiavo made useful suggestions or helped in other ways. Warm thanks go also to Glen Hartley and Lynn Chu of Writers' Representatives, and to Alexis Gargagliano, Molly Dorozenski, Erich Hobbing, and Dan Cuddy of Scribner.

Grateful acknowledgment is made of the magazines in which these poems first appeared and the magazine editors who selected them. A sincere attempt has been made to locate all copyright holders. Unless otherwise noted, copyright to the poems is held by the individual poets.

Kazim Ali: "The Art of Breathing" appeared in *Barrow Street*. Reprinted by permission of the poet.

Jeannette Allée: "Crimble of Staines" appeared in *FIELD*. Reprinted by permission of the poet.

Rae Armantrout: "Scumble" appeared in *American Poet*. Reprinted by permission of the poet.

Mary Jo Bang: "The Opening" appeared in *Verse*. Reprinted by permission of the poet.

Nicky Beer: "Still Life with Half-Turned Woman and Questions" appeared in *Beloit Poetry Journal*. Reprinted by permission of the poet.

Marvin Bell: "The Method" from *Mars Being Red*. Copyright © 2007 by Marvin Bell. Reprinted by permission of the poet and Copper Canyon Press. First appeared in *Crazyhorse*.

Christian Bök: "Vowels" from *Eunoia*. Copyright © 2001 by Christian Bök. Reprinted by permission of the poet and Coach House Press. Also appeared in *New American Writing*.

Louis E. Bourgeois: "A Voice from the City" appeared in *Sentence*. Reprinted by permission of the poet.

Geoffrey Brock: "Flesh of John Brown's Flesh: Dec. 2, 1859" appeared in *Subtropics*. Reprinted by permission of the poet.

Matthew Byrne: "Let Me Count the Ways" appeared in *Poet Lore*. Reprinted by permission of the poet.

Louise Glück: "Archaic Fragment" appeared in *Poetry*. Reprinted by permission of the poet.

Albert Goldbarth: "Stopping by Woods on a Snowy Evening" appeared in *New Letters*. Reprinted by permission of the poet.

Donald Hall: "The Master" appeared in *The American Poetry Review*. Reprinted by permission of the poet.

Mark Halliday: "Best Am Po" appeared in *POOL*. Reprinted by permission of the poet.

Forrest Hamer: "Initiation" from *Rift*. Copyright © 2007 by Forrest Hamer. Reprinted by permission of the poet and Four Way Books. First appeared in *The American Poetry Review*.

Matthea Harvey: "The Future of Terror/Terror of the Future 7" appeared in *BOMB*. Reprinted by permission of the poet.

Robert Hass: "Bush's War" appeared in *The American Poetry Review*. Reprinted by permission of the poet.

Jane Hirshfield: "Critique of Pure Reason" appeared in *Ploughshares*. Reprinted by permission of the poet.

Daniel Johnson: "Do Unto Others" appeared in *Barrow Street*. Reprinted by permission of the poet.

Richard Kenney: "Auguries" appeared in *Southwest Review*. Reprinted by permission of the poet.

Milton Kessler: "Comma of God" from *Free Concert*. Copyright © 2003. Reprinted by permission of Sonia Kessler and Etruscan Books. Also appeared in *Sentence*.

Galway Kinnell: "Hide-and-Seek, 1933" appeared in *Beloit Poetry Journal*. Reprinted by permission of the poet.

Davis Kirby: "Ode to the Personals" appeared in *Five Points*. Reprinted by permission of the poet.

Julie Larios: "What Bee Did" appeared in *The Cortland Review*. Reprinted by permission of the poet.

Brad Leithauser: "A Good List" from *Curves and Angles*. Reprinted by permission of the poet and Alfred A. Knopf. First appeared in *The New Criterion*.

Ben Lerner: "He had enough respect . . ." and "The aircraft rotates . . ." from *Angle of Yaw*. Copyright © 2006 by Ben Lerner. Reprinted by permission of the poet and Copper Canyon Press. First appeared in *Beloit Poetry Journal*.

Joanie Mackowski: "When I was a dinosaur" appeared in *POOL*. Reprinted by permission of the poet.

Amit Majmudar: "By Accident" appeared in *The Antioch Review*. Reprinted by permission of the poet.

Sabrina Orah Mark: "The 10 Stages of Beatrice" appeared in *Conduit*. Reprinted by permission of the poet.

Campbell McGrath: "Ode to the Plantar Fascia" appeared in *POOL*. Reprinted by permission of the poet.

Leslie Adrienne Miller: "On Leonardo's Drawings" ("Aim" and "Wandering Uterus") appeared in *The Kenyon Review*. Reprinted by permission of the poet.

Marilyn Nelson: "Etymology" appeared in *Literary Imagination*. Reprinted by permission of the poet.

Ed Ochester: "Voltaire at Cirey, 1736" from *Unreconstructed: Poems Selected and New*. Copyright © 2007 by Ed Ochester. Reprinted by permission of the poet and Autumn House Press. First appeared in *Barrow Street*.

Meghan O'Rourke: "Peep Show" from *Halflife*. Copyright © 2007 by Meghan O'Rourke. Reprinted by permission of the poet and W. W. Norton. First appeared in *The Kenyon Review*.

Gregory Orr: "Weeping, weeping, weeping, . . ." appeared in *Rattle*. Reprinted by permission of the poet.

Danielle Pafunda: "Dear Pearce & Pearce, Inc." appeared in *Denver Quarterly*. Reprinted by permission of the poet.

Chad Parmenter: "A Tech's Ode to the Genome Computer" appeared in *The Kenyon Review*. Reprinted by permission of the poet.

Susan Parr: "Swooping Actuarial Fauna" and "Ecstatic Cling" appeared in *Alaska Quarterly Review*. Reprinted by permission of the poet.

Peter Pereira: "Nursemaid's Elbow" from *What's Written on the Body*. Copyright © 2007 by Peter Pereira. Reprinted by permission of the poet and Copper Canyon Press. First appeared in *New England Review*.

Robert Pinsky: "Louie Louie" first appeared in *The American Poetry Review*; "Stupid Meditation on Peace" first appeared in *The New Yorker*. Reprinted by permission of the poet.

David Rivard: "The Rev. Larry Love Is Dead" from *Sugartown*. Copyright © 2006 by David Rivard. Reprinted by permission of the poet and Graywolf Press. Also appeared in *TriQuarterly*.

Marya Rosenberg: "If I Tell You You're Beautiful, Will You Report Me?: A West Point Haiku Series" appeared in *Hanging Loose*. Reprinted by permission of the poet.

Natasha Sajé: "F" appeared in *Beloit Poetry Journal*. Reprinted by permission of the poet.